HAUNTED
DAMARISCOTTA

HAUNTED DAMARISCOTTA

GHOSTS OF THE TWIN VILLAGES AND BEYOND

GREG LATIMER

Haunted
America

Published by Haunted America
A Division of The History Press
Charleston, SC 29403
www.historypress.net

First published 2014

Manufactured in the United States

ISBN 978.1.62619.305.5

Library of Congress CIP data applied for.

Dedicated to my wife, Sally. Our first date was an adventure exploring haunts and mysteries, and it seems to have never ended.

CONTENTS

Contents

ACKNOWLEDGEMENTS

Very few things of any consequence can be accomplished by one person alone, and that especially holds true with publishing a book. If it takes a village to raise a child, then it takes at least a good-sized crowd to render a book.

Of course, it's impossible to thank everyone, from the folks who took time out from their day to answer questions from a journalist to those who lent their considerable expertise to make the stories come together in a reasonable, factual form. So first, I would like to thank all of those in this category, too many to mention and giving too much to forget.

Next, I must give my warmest thanks to my wife, Sally, who was not only my invaluable proofreader but also my invaluable partner when it came to encouragement (and, with some items, discouragement) as well as unconditional support for this project. There are many reasons I love her, and every day brings more such reasons.

Then, I need to thank my secondary proofreader, Kathy Lizotte, who was always willing to do more than asked and always capable of doing more than ever expected.

I also want to thank my early supporters who encouraged me to take on the project of writing a book, a far cry from my usual work of writing articles for periodicals. Among these is Jim Runyon, who sometimes saw more in me than I did in myself.

Also among this group is Sonny Pulsifer, whose untimely death I still mourn and who was one of the first locals to encourage me join the community when I moved to Damariscotta some fifteen years ago. Perhaps the greatest compliment he gave me was when he costumed himself for Halloween in a cheap suit and a snap-brim hat as "Scoop Latimer."

And finally among these early supporters is Glenn Chadbourne, who, as Stephen King's illustrator, was kind enough to sell me some illustrations for this book at bargain basement prices.

I also need to thank Chris Roberts and the staff of *The Lincoln County News*, who, for over a decade, have allowed me not just a place of employment but a second family as well. *The Lincoln County News*'s former editor Judi Finn took a chance publishing stories written by a fellow "from away," and current editor Sherwood Olin has been a longtime friend and confidant. Sherwood's wife, Cynthia, has also supported not only journalistic endeavors but a number of public service efforts as well.

And then, of course, it's important to thank the most recent folks who took a chance on me—my commissioning editor Katie Orlando and the crew at The History Press.

Finally, comes "the list" of all those to whom I owe such a debt of gratitude as I finish up my first book, *Haunted Damariscotta*.

Chip Holmes; Graham Walsh; Michael and Lynne Borland; Scott Folsom; Charlie Herrick; Sarah Davison-Jenkins; Peter Everett; Arlene Cole and Nancy Hartley of the Newcastle Historical Society; Calvin and Marjorie Dodge of the Damariscotta Historical Society; Sandi Day; Nicholas Ullos; B.J. Russell; Christine Anderson; Mary Oliveri; the Maurer family; John O'Connell; Dr. Joseph Griffin, DDS; Jeff Pierce; Susan Blagden; and Ralph and Judy Doering.

INTRODUCTION

Do you believe in ghosts? Have you ever seen a chilling apparition float through a misty woods? Or heard heavy footsteps in the darkness of an empty hall?

For most of us, the answer is "no," But for those who answer "yes," there is usually a spine-tingling story sure to follow.

Certainly there is no tale better told than that of a restless spirit on a lonely haunt.

With all its lonely roads, timeworn buildings and historic cemeteries, the Damariscotta area is full of ghost stories. Dating back to the earliest settlers, there were tales of mysterious happenings in the dark woods and on the lonely islands.

After examining many such stories, we have selected the best for your reading pleasure. In each of these, the credibility of the tale was established through careful research and, in many cases, personal interviews.

Readers may have a difference of opinion with the folks interviewed, but the people who told their stories did so with the absolute belief that they were relating the truth as they knew it.

Bill Russell of Round Pond said it best when telling the tale of how his brother was saved by the ghost of his grandfather.

"Halloween is make-believe," Russell said in a deadly serious tone of voice. "This ghost story is for real."

So, find a comfortable old chair by the fireplace, turn down the lights just enough and read on—if you dare—about Haunted Damariscotta.

Damariscotta at dusk. *Photo by Greg Latimer.*

Chapter 1

BURIED ALIVE

After over one hundred years in an unmarked grave, has Mary Howe finally found peace, or does her angry spirit still haunt the community that may have buried her alive?

There are many differences of opinion. In recent times, there have been reports of strange phenomena associated with a house on Hodgdon Street in Damariscotta where, in 1882, Mary Howe spent her last hours aboveground. One report asserts that an exorcism was finally performed on the residence to release her tortured soul. And while these reports remain unconfirmed, and the location of the home will remain unpublished out of respect for the privacy of its present owners, what we do know about Mary Howe is intriguing indeed.

Born in 1831 to Joel and Patty Howe of Damariscotta, Mary was one of nine children in the family. Joel Howe had served with the Second Regiment of Infantry, Seventh Division, of the Militia of Massachusetts during the War of 1812. A graduate of Harvard, Joel had studied military tactics and was elevated to the rank of colonel during the war. When hostilities ended, Colonel Howe resigned his commission and moved his family to Damariscotta, where he bought up a considerable tract of land in the area of present-day Elm and Hodgdon Streets.

The family built the Howe House Inn on Elm Street, a popular venue at the time with guests, including President James K. Polk, who was touring Maine lighthouses. Following the death of Colonel Howe, Mary and her brother Edwin took over operations at the Howe House.

Was Mary Howe buried alive? *Illustration by Glenn Chadbourne.*

They introduced a few new guest attractions, including conversations with the dead.

Spiritualism, a movement based on the belief that spirits of the dead have the ability to communicate with the living, was sweeping the nation. Usually, these communications were facilitated by a medium who gathered guests for a séance.

During the séance, the medium would use trances and other methods to contact the spirit world and often request the spirits to manifest themselves by moving tables, making noises or even speaking out loud. The lyrics of "Spirit Rappings," a popular song in 1853, described noises made during a séance (and was almost certainly not a "rap" song, despite the name).

During the height of its popularity, Spiritualism had more than eight million followers in the United States and Europe, according to an 1897 article in the *New York Times*.

Mary became a spiritualist who specialized in deep trances. She and her brother Edwin hosted popular parties at the Howe House beginning

The Lincoln County Hospital occupying the former Howe House where Mary Howe and her brother Edwin held séances. *Photo courtesy of the Damariscotta Historical Society.*

The Clarks Apartments on Elm Street in Damariscotta have a long and haunted history. Joel Howe constructed the building in 1820 as the Howe House inn and tavern. His daughter Mary held séances there in the mid-1800s. She later went into a trance and may have been buried alive when a local doctor declared her dead. Many years later, the building became Lincoln County Hospital. Current residents of the apartments have described a variety of paranormal manifestations. *Photo by Greg Latimer.*

The front doorway of the Clarks Apartments is decorated with carvings on either side of the entrance done by local shipwrights. *Photo by Greg Latimer.*

in the 1870s in which Mary would call on spirits of the dead to speak with the attendees. Strange noises and ethereal voices were reported by those in the room.

Mary would also "channel" with "the other side," bringing her visions back to the audience with graphic detail. Often such "channeling" would result in a prediction of the future.

In one case, Mary announced that a local man who was visiting New York would never return. The man died that same evening during the lighting ceremony for the Brooklyn Bridge, according to reports in the Castner Files on file at the Skidompha Library in Damariscotta.

The séances continued for over a decade, moving with Edwin and Mary after they sold the Howe House and moved up the road to the house on Hodgdon Street. (It may be noteworthy that many years later, when the former Howe House was being renovated, construction workers found unexplained wires and tubes hidden in the walls, leading some to wonder if these devices may have been used to somehow "enhance" contact with the spirit world.)

A stairway at Clarks Apartments on Elm Street in Damariscotta, a location where séances were held in the 1800s by Mary Howe and where the Lincoln County Hospital (and the morgue) was located from 1930 to 1941. Numerous paranormal manifestations have been reported at the location. *Photo by Greg Latimer.*

It was Mary's practice of going into trances that would finally bring her existence to an end, at least on the earth's surface. During one such apparent trance in 1882, a local doctor declared her dead, leading to several weeks of controversy in the village of Damariscotta.

Under the care of her brother Edwin, Mary had slipped into the trance, settling into a quiet room in the house on Hodgdon Street. The trance continued for over a week, during which Edwin made sure that Mary was attended to with heated stones nearby to keep her warm.

A large number of curious visitors came by to observe Mary in this trance. She was described as having little or no respiration and heartbeat, while her skin stayed a natural color and her limbs remained flexible.

After Mary had remained in the trance for over a week, her condition was the talk of the town. All this attention attracted another visitor, Dr. Robert Dixon, a government-appointed physician. He observed Mary and, shortly thereafter, pronounced her dead.

Mary's brother Edwin was vehement in his protests. Many other residents joined in support of him. The controversy continued to brew, and other doctors were called in, only to agree with Dr. Dixon unanimously.

By now, Mary had been in a trance for several weeks, and Kendall Dunbar, publisher of the *Twin Village Herald*, came by the house to see for himself, bringing his employee (and future wife) Laura Castner.

In later years, Laura was to tell her nephew, local historian Harold Castner, that she personally observed Mary Howe showing more signs of life than death. While her breath and pulse were negligible, her skin was warm to the touch and not ashen in color. There were no apparent signs of rigor mortis or postmortem settling of blood in the tissues. But most importantly, there was no odor associated with a body that the doctors claimed had been dead for over two weeks.

Another of these witnesses was Mary L. Hopkins, who noted in her diary on December 20 that "Mary Howe has been dead since the 12th now and they think she is not dead."

Nonetheless, those in power saw fit to issue an order that the family bury the "dead" woman immediately. This imposition raised the wrath of the public, many of whom strongly believed that the authorities were going to bury a woman alive.

In spite of these protests, Dr. Dixon, assisted by the county sheriff and an undertaker, paid a visit to the house on Hodgdon Street one cold December night. They brought in a wooden coffin, placed Mary into it and nailed the lid solidly shut. They loaded her coffin unceremoniously onto a waiting horse-drawn hearse and proceeded through the empty village streets to an undisclosed graveyard where a grave had been dug by out-of-town gravediggers who didn't know the circumstances of the burial. When these gravediggers learned of the situation, they refused to participate any longer.

Working alone in the chill night, the two county officials lowered the box into the dark pit, covered it with sod and then worked to conceal the grave so that those who believed Mary was living wouldn't try to dig her up.

Mary's passing was noted in a column published in the weekly *Lincoln County News* (now defunct and not associated with the current *The Lincoln County News*). On December 22, 1882, it was reported that "a singular case of death occurred, it being that of Miss Mary Howe." The article further noted that Mary "for 48 hours preceding her undoubted demise had slept much of the time, but at moments of waking manifested a degree of strength and clearness of mind."

The entrance to the Glidden Street cemetery in Newcastle, with gravestones that date from the eighteenth century up to the present time. The cemetery is noteworthy because of a number of unusual memorials located here called "sarcophagi." These grave sites are aboveground stone coffins. It is said that Mary Howe was laid to rest here, underground, in a plain wood coffin provided by the Lincoln County authorities, without ceremony, in an unmarked grave during a secretive late-night burial. The reason for the secrecy was that some townspeople believed she was being buried alive, and officials feared her supporters would try to dig her up. *Photo by Greg Latimer.*

Despite the use of the term "undoubted" with regard to Mary's death, the writer apparently did have some doubts, adding that even though "she was found to have ceased breathing and [was] pronounced dead," she did not display other signs of death. "Strange to say there did not take place those usual changes that are accustomed to follow death; the flesh continued soft, the limbs moved freely and no rigidity was perceptible," the article stated.

To this day, no one seems to know for sure in which graveyard Mary was laid to rest. The name "Glidden" appears in some references to the cemetery, but there are two lots that have used that name. However, the most probable location is the riverside Glidden Street Cemetery, in Newcastle just across the bridge from Damariscotta.

Local residents recall that in their youth, it was a common activity to sneak into the cemetery at night seeking signs of Mary Howe's burial location or paranormal presence. There have been reports of unusual mists drifting through the headstones at night, as well as voices and muffled screams eerily borne on midnight breezes.

Popular myth asserts that unknowing trespassers walking on Mary's hidden grave will suddenly hear hollow echoes of eternal agony rumbling

The Glidden Street Cemetery in Newcastle, where it is rumored that Mary Howe lies in an unmarked grave. *Photo by Greg Latimer.*

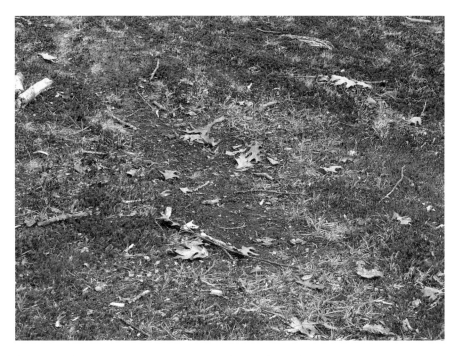

Does this void in the early spring lawn at the Glidden Street Cemetery in Newcastle mark the spot where Mary Howe was laid to rest? And was she still alive when she was buried? *Photo by Greg Latimer.*

up through the very ground under them. But perhaps it is the sensitivities of dogs that best herald the location of Mary's remains, for it said that any dog setting foot over Mary's body will raise its head to the sky and emit a long, lonesome howl.

Chapter 2

A GHOST TO THE RESCUE

Bill Russell of Round Pond tells the story like it was just yesterday of the time his grandfather's ghost appeared and saved the life of his brother Herbert.

This is a tale told by Bill's grandmother and mother, and there is not a member of the family who disbelieves them. As far as any of the Russells are concerned, the event is as factually a part of their family history as any wedding or birthday.

"This isn't some make-believe ghost story," Bill Russell stated with emphasis. "This is a real ghost story."

The story begins on a sunny afternoon in 1932 at the Russell family's Damariscotta residence on Bristol Road.

The man of the house, Herbert Russell Sr., was busy with duties at work and was also the Damariscotta fire chief. His wife, Marion, worked as a secretary at the office of a prominent attorney.

Their son, two-year-old Herbert Jr., was left in the care of his grandmother, Mary, whose husband, William Jones, had passed away some four years prior. According to members of the Russell family, Mary was a solid, no-nonsense woman with little regard for tales of ghosts and spirits.

Herbert was a robust little toddler—he would often try to climb out of his crib, risking injury should he fall to the floor.

To safeguard little Herbert, a harness was fashioned with a crisscross of cords to keep him within the crib's confines. The crib was located in a chamber adjacent to a bedroom, and on this particular afternoon,

Young Herbert Russell Jr., whose life was saved by the ghost of his grandfather. *Photo courtesy of the Russell family.*

Mary was out in an ell that was used as a sitting room. Family members recall that, according to Mary's later description, she was comfortably seated and tending to her knitting.

There were no noises coming from baby Herbert's nearby room, and Mary reasonably assumed that the infant was safely asleep.

The home's stand-up grandfather clock was chiming the arrival of the one o'clock hour, and Mary was just beginning to doze. She was just nodding off when she noticed something in the corner of the room. At first it was barely perceptible, like a mist. Slowly, it started to take form, rising up in height and with features becoming apparent. Mary was now wide-awake, staring with amazement into the corner as the shape continued to develop. As it did so, Mary's fascination turned to horror as she recognized the cadaverous form of her dead husband standing in front of her. According to her description, his corpse showed signs of decay, and he was wearing the same clothing he had been buried in.

For several minutes, she simply stared in disbelief, dropping her knitting to the floor and falling back into her chair. All the symptoms of extreme panic began to set in: she experienced shortness of breath and a cold sweat, and Mary began to feel faint.

Then she also noticed that her husband's spectral features showed signs of concern. He slowly raised his arm and pointed a bony finger at her. As she gazed at the surreal sight, he moved his finger away from her and pointed at the door leading to the baby's chamber, as though directing her to enter the room.

Still controlled by fear, she involuntarily rose from the chair, and as she stepped toward the phantom, it suddenly disappeared with a hissing noise.

Realizing the ghost's obsession with the door to the chamber, she stepped into the baby's room and was shocked into action by the sight of Herbert strangling in the tangled harness and bleeding from his nose.

The cadaverous ghost of Grandpa Jones enters the house and points insistently at the bedroom door, prompting his (still living) wife to check on the grandchild sleeping in the room, saving the life of the child, who was tangled up in cord. *Illustration by Glenn Chadbourne.*

Quickly, she untangled the baby and restored his ability to breathe. Then, taking him in her arms, she turned back toward the sitting room to telephone her daughter for help. It was then that she noticed a strange sight on the usually immaculate floor: a large pile of brown powder where the spectral cadaver had been standing.

According to those who examined it, the powder somewhat resembled dried blood but was much lighter and absolutely dry. After family members and friends regarded the powdery substance, the powder was turned over to several physicians. Their examination of the substance was careful yet inconclusive, according to family members. Unfortunately, the strange material was either lost or disposed of, with none remaining available for examination using modern-day methods.

Mary Jones was reportedly never the same woman again. Her frightening experience continued to haunt her until April 10, 1937, when she, too, passed from life to death.

While the rest of us can never be sure, Mrs. Jones was certainly being truthful about what she saw standing in the corner of the room on that sunny afternoon in 1932. Her subsequent actions, based entirely on directions from the specter, saved the life of her grandson—and those actions are clearly factual.

Moreover, if the dead could be pulled from their graves in cadaverous form to save a life, then certainly they would be compelled to save the life of one of their own descendants.

What is most haunting about this story of "A Ghost to the Rescue"—which may (or may not) be something to think about while drifting off to sleep—is how close the realm of the unexplained may lie to the realm of our own reality.

The specter's apparent knowledge of an immediate event and then the capability to change the outcome by crossing from his world back into ours is perhaps an indication that the two realms exist on a more collateral basis than some of us would be quite comfortable with.

Chapter 3

THE LADY OF LADD'S HILL

Old houses are often home to several generations of a family, but a house in the Ladd's Hill area of Damariscotta Mills may be home for several generations of ghostly inhabitants as well.

According to residents of the home, a variety of hauntings are manifested in a number of intriguing ways—not the least of which includes the sighting of a ghostly "pretty lady" who likes to visit with children.

An examination of old deeds dates the home's construction to the mid-1800s. Many generations of a single family resided in the home until recently, when a young couple with two children moved in as renters. The home's specific location and identities of these residents will not be published out of respect for their privacy.

Ghostly tales of strange activity within the house began many years ago, according to the present owner, whose family resided there for generations. In fact, the observations and events were so commonplace that they were simply considered a part of household life in the residence. One former resident even used to scold the spooks by name for some of their more irritating activities.

According to observations made by a recent owner, who lived in the house for a number of years and who also visited her relatives there prior to her residency, spooky activities ranged from amusing to downright scary. She believes that the "pretty lady" active in the household is Ruth Buzzell, whose family occupied the building in the early 1900s. Another spirit may be that of an elderly gentleman who was a resident there when the house was a home care facility.

The base of Ladd's Hill is graced by this pond, which constitutes the headwaters of the Damariscotta River. It lies between Damariscotta Lake and Great Salt Bay where the water flows into the Damariscotta River and out to the Atlantic. The shack on the shoreline is a smokehouse that is used to cure alewives, a fish that makes a springtime run up the river and into the lake. *Photo by Greg Latimer.*

One of the most common occurrences is the unexplained movement of articles around the house. While many objects seem to be the subject of mysterious travels, there are some favorites, according to the homeowner.

Cups of coffee seem to have a particular attraction for the ghostly residents. According to the owner, a freshly poured cup in the kitchen would often disappear only to be found later in an upstairs bedroom where no one (alive) had been that day. Another favorite object was a hammer that seemed to disappear whenever it was set down while in use, forcing the user to search the house in frustration in order to finish the work.

The owner also described how the resident spooks helped to watch over a sickly aunt who was bedridden and lived at the house for some time. A particular crocheted blanket would invariably end up covering the aunt on many mornings, regardless of where it had been the night before. This was particularly frustrating to the homeowner's son, who

Ladd's Hill Road (which ironically is a dead end) is in the quaint community of Damariscotta Mills. (Note: The Buzzell residence is not included in this view out of respect for the current residents' privacy.) *Photo by Greg Latimer.*

sometimes went to sleep with the blanket covering him and awakened cold—only to find that the blanket was now warming his aunt.

Lately, the ghostly interest in objects seems to have modernized a bit. Recently, residents reported that a *Harry Potter* DVD that the family had been looking forward to viewing mysteriously disappeared from the laundry room. The whole family joined in a thorough search for the DVD, but the evening ended in frustration. Several days later, the DVD reappeared under a resident's pillow.

One must consider that if some entity is responsible for these disappearances, it must be capable of dry wit, as each of the missing objects was a source of frustration with its loss.

Another common event is the sound of a bouncing ball on the floor of an upstairs bedroom. The owner said that late at night, when all was still in the house, the distinct sound of a ball being repeatedly bounced from the floorboards was a regular occurrence. Each time, the bedroom was unoccupied.

While some may assume that such an activity might be attributed to the ghost of a child, the owner disagrees. Instead, she suspects that the activity may be that of a childlike adult whose spirit may yet remain in the house.

The owner bases this theory on the fact that the house once offered residential services for the elderly. The upstairs area of the house was the dormitory for these patients. One of the patients was an older man whose personality had become childlike with the frailty of age.

Although the man's condition could be considered a handicap, the owner has many fond memories of him, recalling how he loved to play with children and join in their games. The old man's favorite pastime was playing ball with the children, according to the homeowner.

One Christmas morning, when the patients were awakened to open their presents, the old man was found to have died in his sleep. From that time on, the lonely sound of a single bouncing ball moving across the floor and through walls that had recently been added to the house became commonplace.

Recent residents say that they regularly hear the distinct sound as well, even though the room was occupied by their children. When they would go upstairs to check on the noise, the children were always fast asleep. Moreover, their bedroom toy collection does not include a ball.

Ladd's Hill is located in the historic and scenic Damariscotta Mills area where an annual run of small fish called "alewives" occurs every spring. Running along the right side of this photo of the millpond are sluices that have been used to harvest the fish since the 1800s. It is thought that the annual alewife run may be the source for the name "Damariscotta," which is said to mean "place of many small fishes" in the Native American Abenaki language. *Photo by Greg Latimer.*

Ruth Buzzell shown in an undated photo. Could this be the ghostly Lady of Ladd's Hill in earthly form? Family members who have lived in the residence believe that many of the manifestations at her former home can be attributed to her, and two children described a visit from an apparitional "pretty lady" who resembled Buzzell. *Photo courtesy of Mary Oliveri.*

Despite the long history of strange occurrences, the most compelling event took place only several years ago. It involved the two young children and a visit from a friendly spirit that the children called "the pretty lady."

The incident took place while the couple was downstairs preparing the family dinner, and the children were upstairs, apparently at play.

When dinner was ready, the mother went to the stairway and summoned the children. Then she began placing plates on the table. Several minutes later, the children still hadn't arrived for dinner. The mother again loudly called out for them. This time, the children came down the stairs, ready for dinner and with smiles on their faces.

Irritated over the children's delay and their apparent disregard for her urging them to dinner, the mother inquired about what had kept them upstairs.

The children replied quite matter-of-factly that they had been talking with a pretty lady upstairs. While somewhat astounded, the adults were convinced that the "pretty lady" was most certainly a childhood fantasy—until they took the children upstairs separately.

Both children described the "pretty lady" in exactly the same manner and pointed out exactly the same location for her appearance. Since neither child seemed to be adversely affected by the experience, the parents decided to let the incident pass without further discussion.

Children visit with ghostly Lady of Ladd's Hill in their upstairs bedroom. Both children described the apparition as a "pretty lady" and said they enjoyed the visit. *Illustration by Glenn Chadbourne.*

Many questions still remain unanswered about the house on Ladd's Hill and its apparent collection of unearthly residents. As the mysterious appearances and reappearances of objects continue and the sound of a ghostly ball sometimes echoes in the night, the mortal residents still wonder who the "pretty lady" might be and when she might appear again.

While the adults admit to some fear of the spooky goings on, the children remain unaffected, even entertained by the events. It all leads one to wonder about the openness of a child's mind, the playful antics of some resident spooks and a friendly visit from the mysterious Lady of Ladd's Hill.

Chapter 4

MYSTERY SHIP OF THE DECEMBER STORM

A full-rigged barkentine ship, adrift and crewless off Seguin Island in a raging December storm. A young ship captain beating homeward through gale-force winds, trying to reach Newcastle in time for his wedding. And an intrepid reporter who years later told the story of a maritime mystery that has yet to be solved.

All of these elements come together in this classic tale of the sea, those who sail upon it, those who wait for them on shore and the mysterious fate of an entire ship's crew. And all of it is well-documented fact.

The story begins at the ending—in 1876—when Kendall Dunbar, editor of the *Damariscotta Village Herald and Record*, made his way to the home of an old seafarer, Captain George Nickels of Newcastle.

Dunbar was always looking for a good story, and he had heard around the riverside wharves of how Captain Nickels had succeeded in an adventure many years prior. While known as a man eager to cover the news, Dunbar was also regarded as accurate and credible in his writing. In later years, he would be elected president of the Maine Press Association.

And so it was that Kendall Dunbar sat down with the elderly Captain Nickels at his home overlooking the Damariscotta River. The old sea captain, now widowed and with his seafaring sons away on voyages, stoked his pipe and stared wistfully out his window.

Slowly he puffed, and as fragrant smoke filled his well-appointed sitting room, he told a story that Dunbar copied verbatim, right down to the seaman's language used by the old skipper. Even though Nickels spoke in the dry, understated style of a veteran Yankee skipper, the reporter was barely able to contain his amazement as the story unfolded.

After the interview, Dunbar quickly rushed to his office on Main Street, turned the oil lamps up bright and wrote until four o'clock that morning. His published story is still preserved on yellowed pages of the *Village Herald and Record*, on file at the Lincoln County Courthouse in Wiscasset.

The captain began his tale by describing a festive birthday party at the home of the Sherman family in North Edgecomb in the early fall days of October 1821. One of the family's daughters, a vivacious young woman named Mary, had been George's first and only love. As partygoers prepared to serve homemade ice cream and birthday cake, George and Mary quietly left the room and were gone for some time. They returned just as the cake was to be served, their faces beaming with happy smiles.

As Mary's mother succeeded in blowing out all but two of the candles on her birthday cake, she commented that the two remaining candles must symbolize George and Mary, whose love could not be extinguished.

It was at that moment that George proudly rose from the table and announced his marriage proposal to Mary and her acceptance. George told the enthusiastic crowd that his intentions were to fulfill his obligations as a ship's captain and make a scheduled trip to Barbados and then to marry upon his return in December of that year.

The following day, Captain Nickels stood tall aboard the quarterdeck of the schooner *Maria*, issuing orders to the crew in preparation for departure from the Newcastle wharves. With her friends and family, Mary stood on the dock and blew her betrothed a final kiss.

As the little two-masted "coaster" sailed downriver, George used his telescope to look shoreward. There he had his parting view of Mary as she eagerly waved a white handkerchief toward the departing vessel.

The run to Barbados went smoothly. The cargo of lumber was unloaded, and a return cargo of sugar, molasses and rum were stowed away in the *Maria*'s holds. Departing the island port, *Maria* sailed north into increasingly stormy weather—and a meeting with mystery.

They made Hatteras in good time and started counting the days until they would reach home. Captain Nickels was optimistic about arriving by the scheduled date for his wedding. His first mate, Mr. Fossett, was eager to return home to Bristol and tend to his wife, who had taken ill. The rest of the crew looked forward to being home with loved ones for the holiday.

As the crew began to recognize landmarks along the Maine coast, a watch was set to look for Seguin Island, the landmark that would allow the helmsman to lay a course for Boothbay and the mouth of the Damariscotta River. The crew remained eager for home, but the weather was beginning to work even harder against them.

"Cold!" was the Yankee skipper's succinct description, as transcribed by Kendall Dunbar. "Wind was west an' no'th, and when [the spray] struck anywhere's aboard, w'al there it froze," he recalled.

"The old schooner was all iced up for'ard, and what with the wind a'haulin' further to the nor'ard all the time, an' it a lookin' nasty in the nor' west; I had about made up my mind that we couldn't get into the mouth of the Dam'iscotty River, so's to be home on time," Captain Nickels told Dunbar as the reporter scribbled notes furiously.

Sunrise on December 16 found the first mate Mr. Fossett aloft in the rigging, keeping an eye out for Seguin Island. The weather had worsened, limiting visibility, but Fossett was known for his sharp eyesight.

Fossett hadn't been aloft for long when he sang out, "Land ho!" And then, after only a moment's hesitation, added in near disbelief, "Sail ho!"

Incredulous at the thought of another vessel bearing from the north under these conditions, Captain Nickels shouted back, "Where away?"

"Just to the south'rd of Seguin, Cap'n," Fossett shouted from his perch in the rigging.

While the mast swayed wildly with the ocean's cresting waves, Fossett strained his eyes into the storm. What he saw caused him to shout back in surprise, "It's a bark sir…Under tops'ls…An' she's a wanderin' in her course!"

The captain explained to the landsman reporter that a large three-masted vessel such as a barkentine was seldom seen so close to shore north of Portland. Additionally, the setting of her topsails, top-most on the masts, was somewhat unusual for the conditions. Her "wandering" course meant that her heading kept changing, which was especially unusual in that most ships at sea follow a fairly straight course, especially in foul weather.

As Fossett continued to shout down updates on the bark's position, Captain Nickels retrieved his telescope. Extending the spyglass, he directed it toward the area Fossett was pointing. Bracing himself steady against the pounding sea, he found the ship in his sights and brought the strange vessel into focus.

"She was a'yarrin, and a pitchin' 'round in a curious fashion," the captain related, "and her ensign was run straight up the mizzen." The ensign (a flag identifying a ship's owner) seemed unusually placed, and after some time, Nickels was able to see something about it that caused him some real concern.

The flag was flying upside down, an international sign of distress.

Nickels then described to Dunbar the scene surrounding him on the *Maria*'s frozen decks.

The sturdy little schooner was struggling valiantly against the sea. Mr. Fossett, still in the frozen rigging, was hanging on like a desperate cat as the mast swung to and fro. The excited crew was slipping and sliding over the pitching deck, making their way to grasp the icy rails and get a better view of the mystery ship.

All of them wanted to be home in time for Christmas, especially the captain with his wedding plans. None of them wanted to perish in this storm, attempting the dangerous rescue of a much larger vessel.

The full rigged ship *B.F. Metcalf* shown moored at Jack's Wharf on the Newcastle side of the Damariscotta River. This vessel serves as an example of what the December storm mystery ship may have looked like, with that ship being described as a full-rigged barkentine—a three-masted ship like this one. An observer can easily see how challenging it must have been for the crew of the *Maria* to scramble from a small rowboat up the sides of ship like this one in the middle of a raging ice storm. This particular ship was built in Damariscotta at the Metcalf Shipyard on Water Street and launched on September 30, 1875. She was 180 feet long with a beam of 35 feet and a depth of 23 feet, weighing in at 1,050 tons. She was described at the time as one of the largest and finest vessels ever built in Damariscotta. As was so common in the age of sail, she was lost with all hands some years later during a passage from Java. *Photo courtesy of the Damariscotta Historical Society.*

But they were seamen, and as Captain Nickels explained, "There was a vessel to wind'ard in distress, and a sailor can't stand for that—for he don't ever know how soon it may be his own turn."

Captain Nickels ordered Mr. Fossett down from the rigging and had his helmsman set a course for the stricken vessel. As the *Maria* closed distance on the barkentine, the crew began noticing more disturbing sights about the vessel.

"Somethin' seems wrong with her steering gear," the sharp-eyed Mr. Fossett observed. "An' see how strange she's working; first her tops'ls all full an' then comin' up into the wind so 'at they all go slack."

Then the helmsman, an old sailor named Lewett, stared through the storm and made an observation more chilling than the sea spray that frosted his oilskins. "'Pears to me," he said, narrowing his eyes against the wind, "tha's not a soul aboard that ship."

Sure enough, as the crew stared in disbelief, there was no sign of life aboard the barkentine. Her windswept quarterdeck was without an officer in command or a helmsman to lay the course. Her rails, cased in ice, were vacant of passengers or crew. No one appeared from below decks to welcome rescuers as they closed in on the vessel with a distress signal posted atop her mizzenmast.

As they drew within hailing distance, their calls went unanswered. Her rigging appeared to be of foreign design, and there was no name painted on her bow or stern.

As the sailors tried to locate the barkentine's lifeboats, either ready in davits or lashed to the deck, they could see none. Captain and crew began to realize that some strange fate had befallen this vessel, and they prepared to board her and find out what it might be.

The men knew that even in the best of weather, boarding an unmanned ship that was also underway would be somewhat risky. In a full gale, such as the one that engulfed them, it would be clearly dangerous.

But there was always a possibility that there was someone still alive but incapacitated on board, and if indeed the vessel was abandoned, there would be money for her salvage. But all of this might come at a cost. At best, they might not make it home by Christmas. At worst, some of them might not make it home—ever.

The little schooner *Maria* only carried a crew of seven, which had been bolstered to eight with the addition of a sailor in Barbados who offered to work his way home.

The captain assembled his crew and, shouting over the scream of wind in the rigging, he laid out his plan. "Now, Mr. Fossett," he told his second in

The coasting schooner *Lois Candage,* shown under full sail in this undated photo, offers a version of what the schooner *Maria* would have looked like. Compared with a barkentine like the December storm mystery ship, she was considerably smaller. Her length was fifty-nine feet with a beam of nineteen feet, six inches and a depth of six feet, five inches. She was built in 1912 and continued to ply the waters of coastal Maine until the early 1980s, when she was permanently tied up in Damariscotta. There she fell into disrepair and settled into an area between Schooner Landing and the Municipal Parking Lot in Damariscotta known as "Misery Gulch," where sections of her hull still protrude above the mud at low tide. Her rudder was salvaged and is on display in the Schooner Landing parking lot. *Photo courtesy of the Damariscotta Historical Society.*

command, "Take the schooner and lay to, an' when we get far enough to wind'ard; get the stern boat ready to put over.

"If you think you can handle the old *Maria* between two men an' yourself," he told the first mate, "then I'll take four men an' myself, an' get that bark in somewhere's.

"We was all excited," Captain Nickels said. "We knew if we could anyway work her into a harbor, we could make a big thing on the salvage money; an' we was all of us, what you might call poor men, so two or three thousand dollars apiece was worth runnin' a good deal of risk for."

So they positioned the schooner and lowered her stern boat according to plan. "And such a time we had," the Yankee skipper said. "For the sea was runnin' fearful high, an' it was a full job for one man just to keep the boat from fillin' with water by bailin' fast as he could—an' the water was colder n' anything this side o' the North Pole."

When they finally came alongside the bark, she was so high off the water, and the storm waves so violent, that the brave group of men in the rowboat wasn't sure if they could board her at all. With the huge vessel lifting in and out of the angry sea and ocean water spilling from her tall decks like a waterfall after each wave, the crew desperately maneuvered the small boat closer.

A particularly stout crewman by the name of Poole, who Nickels described as a "master feller to handle himself," volunteered to try scrambling aboard the pitching barkentine.

"That bark was yawin' 'round so; but Poole, he just watched for his chance," Captain Nickels said. "When the vessel rolled the right way, well Poole gave a mighty jump" and was the first of the men able to scramble aboard the mystery ship.

Making the rowboat's bow line fast to the bark's stern, the rest of the sailors were able to board as well, and there they found more questions than answers.

A quick search confirmed that all the bark's lifeboats were indeed missing, and there was no one aboard.

Fearing that the ship was abandoned because she was sinking, the crew quickly checked below decks. The pumps were in working order, and there was only thirteen inches of water in her bilge. There were no serious leaks to be found.

The crew also found the reason for the barkentine's seemingly erratic course. Her wheel had been lashed down, and with her topsails set and providing steerage, her course was a huge circle that drifted slowly to leeward. Before searching any further, the sailors had to concern themselves with putting the ship on some course. At present, their greatest concern affecting that objective was the heavy weather that surrounded them.

Calling on a crewman named Joe Tharber, whom the captain described as better than a barometer for weather forecasting, Nickels asked what to expect for the coming night.

"Wind a comin' from the nor'ard and east'ard tonight," said the salty old Tharber. "An' it's a goin' to blow some too." Captain Nickels looked over his new command and took action to safeguard her. He decided to "hove to," which is to close all hatches, leave a small sail up for steerage and ride out the storm.

First he ordered his small crew to climb the rigging and stow the topsails on the main and mizzenmasts, leaving one up for steerage on the foremast.

A particularly stout crewman by the name of Poole, described as a "master feller to handle himself," volunteered to try scrambling aboard the pitching barkentine. *Illustration by Glenn Chadbourne.*

Because the crew was so small, each sail had to be done one at a time, with the group of men struggling up the two masts to secure the sails.

Then Nickels assigned a crewman named Hartley Thorpe to man the helm. With only one sail up, Nickels said the bark "laid easy as a duck and stayed tol'able dry."

With the vessel secure, the small group of men had time to explore further, and what they found left them in awe. "My eyes!" the captain exclaimed later as he described the plush salon and velvet covered lounges and chairs.

The cabin walls were graced with expensive oil paintings and large mirrors. In one end of the cabin was a crucifix and altar. In another cabin, a library full of books awaited someone to read them. A stringed musical instrument lay abandoned on the floor.

Tharber, the crewman with a good sense for the weather, was apparently adept at other perceptions. As he looked through some elegantly designed chests and took in the well-appointed surroundings, he raised an eyebrow and announced, "Been women folk here, sure 'nough."

The only hint of trouble was an overturned worktable, something that could have happened due to the storm. None of the veteran seamen could understand why the vessel had been abandoned.

The log of the bark's captain was recovered but written in French, which none of the men could read. From the few words they could understand, it appeared that the ship's cargo was part silks and part wine, and that her home port was somewhere in the Mediterranean.

Outside, the storm screeched and howled. The angry ocean sent its waves crashing against the bark's solid timbers. Above decks at the helm, Hartley Thorpe stood his lonely vigil, guiding the ship to safety. Below decks, a small group of hardy seamen tried to understand a story they would never be able to know for sure: what had happened to the seafarers whose footsteps had preceded theirs in this luxurious cabin.

"It made us feel pitiful like," Captain Nickels later told Kendall Dunbar. "To see all that beautiful stuff, an' know that most likely the people who owned it was at the bottom of the sea."

When dawn came on December 18, the storm had calmed. The wind became southwesterly, and the crew went to work putting up more sail. They sighted Seguin Island by noon and took a bearing for Boothbay.

Captain Nickels stood at the rail of the bark's quarterdeck, his eyes ranging westward ahead of the ship's bow. Westward, to home—and to Mary. With a little luck, he still might make his wedding date, which was set for that very same day.

At six o'clock that evening, Captain Nickels dropped the mystery ship's anchor in Boothbay Harbor. While the locals gazed in awe at the unusually large ship in their tiny port, Captain Nickels quickly made his way to shore and hired a horse and coach to speed him up the road to Newcastle.

When he reached Bryant's Tavern, the first man he saw was his trustworthy first mate Mr. Fossett, who reported that the *Maria* was safely docked at Jack's Wharf in Newcastle. Having secured both vessels under his command, the captain quickly found a horse and rode at a gallop toward North Edgecomb.

As the tired horse pounded into the Shermans' dooryard, the captain quickly swung out of the saddle and jumped to the ground. Running to the door, he was greeted by Mary, who nearly fainted at the sight of him.

While the family celebrated the sea captain's return, some children of the house dashed off and summoned the minister. Others went to fetch old Uncle Arad Burnham with his fiddle and bring Aunt Abigail Dodge to play the organ.

With everyone in attendance, Aunt Abigail took her place at the organ (which was missing two notes and slightly out of tune) while Uncle Arad struck his fiddle beside her. Together, they played what must have been one of the most unusual bridal marches ever rendered.

At nine o'clock in the evening of December 18, 1821, Captain George Nickels and Miss Mary Sherman were wed, just as promised. The mysterious barkentine was delivered to Boston for salvage, and a bit more was learned about her.

According to shipping sources there, it was the ship's maiden voyage, and she had sailed out of Marseilles, France. Even more unnerving to the newlywed Captain Nickels was the revelation that the bark's captain, a young Frenchman, had sailed from port with his own newlywed wife on their honeymoon. Nothing was ever heard of what fate may have befallen the young couple and the ship's crew.

Captain Nickels and his crew were paid a handsome reward in salvage money, but it's doubtful any of them ever forgot the heavy air of tragedy aboard that abandoned ship, the frightful storm they braved to recover her and the still unsolved mystery that they discovered.

Chapter 5

THE LEGEND OF JOHNNY ORR'S

Did the ghost of a pirate lead an honest shipwright to a fortune in ill-begotten gold? And was the shipwright then lost to treacherous river currents, or did he simply slip out of town?

These are the questions surrounding a dangerous bend in the Damariscotta River, where the tidal waters run fast through the rocky shallows. Through the efforts of a diligent reporter in the 1800s, and those of a local historian in the 1900s, the legend of Johnny Orr's is a tale still told in the twin villages of Damariscotta and Newcastle.

The mystery also begins with a mystery: how did the name Johnny Orr's (also called Johnny Orr) come to be bestowed on a narrows in the Damariscotta River about midway between the Newcastle/Damariscotta Bridge and the Great Salt Bay?

To be certain, the name has nothing to do with the well-known college basketball coach John Michael "Johnny" Orr, who led teams in Wisconsin, Michigan and Iowa from the late 1950s through the mid-1990s.

It is also unlikely that "Johnny Orr" was the name of a Native American or a name that settlers had given a Native American, as was the case with "Chief Robinhood" in the nearby Five Islands area of Sagadahoc County or "Chief Jack Pudding" in the Newcastle area.

Most local historians agree that Johnny Orr was probably an early settler who may have perished in the rapids sometime during the very early history of Damariscotta. Some say he could have been a pirate. The name appears on old charts and in some early records. It is mentioned specifically in a

Johnny Orr's, a bend in the Damariscotta River with the towns of Newcastle and Damariscotta on opposite riverbanks. The river is tidal, and when the outgoing and incoming currents roll through the narrows at Johnny Orr's, the area is awash with whitewater. A fortune in gold was said to be plucked out from under a rock in these narrows after a man was led there by dreams of a ghostly pirate. *Photo by Greg Latimer.*

poem written in 1857 entitled "To the River Damaiscotta" (his spelling), by nineteen-year-old Newcastle resident Edward Kavanagh Gazet. He describes the rushing tide, the oyster banks, the roaring falls and the bend of "Johnny Orr." (Gazet later joined Company A, Eleventh Regiment Massachusetts Volunteers during the Civil War, where he saw action in several battles until he succumbed from either illness or injuries at Fortress Monroe Hospital, Virginia, in 1862.)

There are tales told in historical texts and local anecdotes of a former pirate named Johnny Orr who resided in Newcastle during his waning years. Orr was said to make mysterious nocturnal visits to the Damariscotta River shoreline—in particular, to the narrows that would bear his name. There is some speculation that the old pirate was swept away by the currents and taken by the river, never to be seen again, during one of these nighttime forays.

Our story of Johnny Orr's begins in 1850 when a local shipwright named Ralph Mortland began to have a series of strange dreams involving a ghostly pirate figure and a treasure hidden under the treacherous rapids at Johnny Orr's. Was the spirit of the old pirate calling from behind the dark curtain of death for the young shipwright to recover his lost treasure, using dreams as a way to communicate? That is one aspect of this story, among others, that may never be known. It is for this reason that, in spite of the many documented facts, our tale is still known as the "legend" of Johnny Orr's.

Ralph was well regarded in the community as an industrious and intelligent young man. His skills as a shipwright were well appreciated, and he also had a knack for analyzing and improving various systems. In one case, he created a plan to simplify the cost records of ships under construction at the many wharves in Damariscotta and Newcastle, making it much easier to compute expenditures on material.

He lived with his widowed mother, Mary, in a small wood-frame house on the Damariscotta side of the river and enjoyed a simple life.

The residents of Damariscotta and Newcastle well recalled the tragic accident in which Ralph Mortland apparently fell out of a small boat he was using to explore the river near Johnny Orr's and was subsequently swept to his death by the currents and perhaps out to sea. A thorough search of the shoreline on both banks of the Damariscotta River was made, and no clue to Mortland's fate could be discerned. The only evidence located was the small boat Mortland had apparently been in, tied off to a sapling near Johnny Orr's.

Mortland's grieving mother was inconsolable, so it was no great surprise that when she received a letter some months after the apparent drowning, she immediately packed her belongings and left her tiny house, purchasing a stage ticket to New York City and boarding the next southbound coach.

Curious neighbors soon started gossiping, and it was learned that the letter lacked a return address except for the words "Havana, Cuba." It also seemed exceedingly thick, as though packed with something.

The Mortland family was soon forgotten by most of the community, but not by a young reporter named Everett Dunbar who wrote for a small newspaper in town called the *Advertiser* (the predecessor of the *Twin Villages Herald and Record*). It wasn't until 1875 that Dunbar was able to travel to New York, officially for a holiday concert, but his real mission was to locate Mary Mortland in an effort to discover the truth behind Ralph's disappearance and his mother's exit from town.

Dunbar's detailed account of this story, published in 1876, and additional research done by local historian Harold Castner in the 1950s have allowed the following incredibly detailed documentation of this legend.

Dunbar was secretive about his methods and what resources he was able to utilize on his quest. His published story describes finding a lead that took him to the doorstep of a "palatial residence" somewhere on Fifth Avenue in

New York City. A knock on the door brought a butler to the entryway. When asked if this was the residence of a Mrs. Mary Mortland, the butler reacted with believable surprise and stated he had never heard the name. Dunbar then asked about Ralph Mortland and tried several other inquiries, all of which the butler answered in the negative.

Disappointed, Dunbar turned from the door and was walking down the front steps when a carriage with both a coachman and footman pulled up. An elderly woman was helped down from coach by the footman, and Dunbar greeted her in the fashion of the day. When he saw her face, he felt there was something familiar about her but couldn't quite place it. When the lady asked if he had business at the house, he replied that he was looking for Mary Mortland. This brought a surprised reaction from the woman, who took a quick, nervous look around her, calmed herself and invited Dunbar into the home, saying that she wanted to learn more about the story he was covering.

When they entered the spacious reception hall, the butler took their coats and hats and led them to a well-furnished sitting room. After being seated, the woman pulled a cord hanging from the ceiling to summon a maid, who returned shortly with hot tea and biscuits. Once the two had settled into their chairs, the woman turned to Dunbar and said, "Now young man, tell me about you. Where do you live, and what is the story of this Mary Mortland?"

Dunbar told her about his family in Damariscotta and his work for the *Advertiser*, which was published by his brother Kendall. He went on to tell the tale of Ralph's disappearance, followed by the exit of Mary Mortland. Although he had never met Ralph or Mary, he had learned of the story and the mysterious package that arrived at the Mortland house, apparently causing Mrs. Mortland to depart for New York City. That was the lead he followed that brought him to New York City and that somehow caused him to learn of the residence on Park Avenue.

According to Dunbar's story, the woman now leaned forward in her chair and looked him directly in the eye. "Wait," she said. "That is enough. I knew your father, and for that reason, I believe you to be an honest and upright young man. I will make you a bargain; I will tell you the truth behind the story you are seeking, and you will promise to never tell the secret of who I am now, who my son is now and where we live. The rest of the story, you are free to tell, and I hope it will give some comfort to the good residents of Damariscotta and Newcastle."

Dunbar was astounded. Could it be possible that he was about to solve a great mystery? "Who are you?" he asked reflexively. "How did you know my father?"

"That will have to wait until after I have your promise," the woman replied.

"I have always been a man of my word," Dunbar said. "If you can help me with the background of this story or aid me in the solution, I will be happy to pledge my word of secrecy for as long as I live."

The old woman eyed Dunbar with a long questioning look, and then she seemed to find the answer she was looking for. She settled back into her chair and took a long sip from her cup of tea. Looking up at Dunbar with a firm gaze, she said, "I am Mary Mortland, and this home belongs to my son, Ralph. We both live under new names, and there is a long and dramatic chain of events that brought us here. Before we part ways this afternoon, you will know the whole story."

With that, she reached again for the cord and summoned her maid to bring a fresh pot of tea.

According to Mrs. Mortland's account, it all began with the strange dreams Ralph Mortland had for three nights in succession.

For the first two nights, the dreams were essentially the same. It was nighttime on the Damariscotta River between the tides, when the river was at its lowest depth and her waters were still and silent, awaiting the incoming tide. Ralph's dreams started with same scene: a small, pallid and frail man aboard a small boat quietly dipping his oars as he moved from the village upriver to Johnny Orr's. He wore the clothes of a common seaman but glanced suspiciously around him with the nervous eyes of a criminal, perhaps a pirate. Tucked away under the seat of his small boat was something perhaps even more piratical: a small but sturdy oaken chest encircled with bands of iron.

Ralph had later told his mother that the man looked more like a ghost than a living man, his pale features sometimes blurred and misty.

The wraith-like figure continued to quietly row the boat upriver until he reached the bend at Johnny Orr's, where he beached the dinghy on the Newcastle side of the river. In his dreams, Ralph watched the man take the chest and wade out into the river to a large rock located about midway from the shore and an island in the river. Even with the low tide, there was enough depth and current to make it hard going for the pale man as he stumbled over the slippery rocks with the heavy chest.

Once he reached the rock, he took the chest and disappeared under the water's surface. He was underwater so long that Ralph was concerned that he may have drowned, but sure enough, his skull-like head finally broke the surface of the water, where he gasped for air. He was no longer carrying

This rock, exposed by a going tide at Johnny Orr's, matches the description of the rock where Ralph Mortland's dreams of a pirate wraith led him to a treasure-trove of gold bars, according to the legend of Johnny Orr's. It is surrounded by dangerous, fast-moving currents that must have challenged Mortland as he removed the gold bars from under the rock and placed them in a small boat, all in the dead of night. *Photo by Greg Latimer.*

the chest. With obvious effort, the frail man made his way to shore and regained his boat, pushing it out into the river and silently rowing back to the sleeping village.

Ralph scarcely regarded this first dream, believing it to be just another nocturnal fantasy. Then he had exactly the same dream the next night. That left him wondering as he headed to work at Day's Shipyard on the Damariscotta wharves that morning.

All day long, he continued to wonder. Why had he been able to see the actions of the ghostly figure so clearly? Why were the proceedings of the first dream so perfectly duplicated in the second dream?

Whenever he dismissed himself as a simpleton for considering such ideas, a powerful feeling that he was witnessing a rare and strange coincidence overwhelmed him and left an impression on his mind that he was dealing with a half-defined mystery.

He was also impressed with the sly and cautious nature of the thin man. Was he a criminal, a pirate? Or was he simply trying to hide a treasure that was rightfully his? Perhaps more ominously, was he actually a living thing, or an apparition from somewhere unknown?

As Ralph settled into bed that night, he was hoping that perhaps he had seen the end of these dreams, with their sense of mystery.

When the dream began on that third night, Ralph could sense an immediate change from the prior two dreams. A terrific gale seemed to be forming up, and the frail man seemed more excited and nervous than in the first two dreams. Ralph also noticed that the man was muttering in low, nearly inaudible tones. Several times, he was able to distinguish some of the phrases. "My last night…Can I secrete this without discovery?" were two of the phrases Ralph was able to hear.

As before, the ghostly man silently rowed his boat to Johnny Orr's and beached it on shore. Also as before, he laboriously lifted yet another small chest, heavy again apparently with more treasure, and stumbled out into the river toward the rock. Stopping there, he once again submerged near the rock, taking with him the new load of treasure. He remained underwater for some time as the stormy winds began to roil the surface water and whip up whitecaps. Then, in his dream, Ralph noticed that the tide began to rise, and a cold hail began to fall on the river, causing tiny splashes where it hit the surface. Still, there was no sign of the frail man.

In his dream, Ralph was beginning to feel that the ghostly man had been taken by the river, when suddenly there was a commotion at the surface as the man's head broke through, desperately gasping for air, his eyes wide with fright.

Ralph continued to dream that as the tide rose and the storm continued to build, the man struggled against the current to regain the shore. He had either placed his treasure chest under the rock or lost it to the tide, and both of his arms flailed against the strength of the incoming tide.

He had almost passed halfway when the current was pressed between two rocks and formed a giant eddy. The whirling vortex surrounded the desperate man. He gasped for breath as the water engulfed him, and his skinny arms seemed to reach for shore as he tried to swim free of the vortex that was now sucking him into its depths. With a final surge of strength, he made a bid for the shore, and it looked like he had made some progress, until the current slowly, inexorably pulled him back into the river depths.

His arms like a windmill, water flying from his wet hair and his eyes like white saucers staring from the river surface into the night sky, the man's mouth opened wide and he emitted a long, high-pitched, pitiful scream that ended in a gurgle as he was pulled down to his death in the cold, dark waters.

Ralph awoke with a start. Outside, he could hear a storm rumbling, and something else: the far-off scream of a human in distress emanating from somewhere upriver. He jumped from his bed and went to the window. Opening it, he took the storm full in his face. He leaned out into the weather and listened intently, hearing nothing but the storm and rush of the river current. He shook his head to clear his thoughts and listened again.

Had he really heard that unholy wail? Or was it part of his dream? A cold sweat was standing out on his brow. Slowly, he closed the window and locked it shut against the wind. He wiped the sweat off his forehead with the sleeve of his nightshirt, and his gaze slowly fell to the floor in front of him as he wondered what was going on.

When he finally returned to bed, it was with a sense of resolve. He was going to borrow a boat and make his way to Johnny Orr's, and if possible, he was going to find a way to search underwater near the mysterious rock in the river.

Ralph proceeded to work the next morning, never mentioning his dreams to either his mother or friends.

The next day, a Saturday, Ralph planned out his venture to Johnny Orr's. Even though he was a strong swimmer, he wasn't anxious to risk the currents around the mysterious rock, so he used his superior skills at craftsmanship and invention. Taking some short wooden planks, he constructed a small box and then placed a pane of glass at one end of it, sealing the edges so it was watertight. He was hoping to use it as a viewer so he could see underwater from the relative safety of a boat. That night he enjoyed a sound sleep, free from troubling dreams of ghostly men and pirate gold.

On Sunday, he awoke earlier than usual in order to catch the daytime tide at its lowest. His mother was a bit surprised and became curious, especially when she learned he wouldn't be attending church. Unable to mislead his mother, Ralph told her of his dreams about the pallid man and of his plan to investigate the area around Johnny Orr's.

Mrs. Mortland considered the effort a fun adventure for her son that would almost certainly lead to nothing but a sunburn from the midday heat and a good story to tell the grandchildren she hoped to have someday. After breakfast, she bid her son good-bye, adding (in good-humored jest) that she hoped he would find the treasure.

Ralph walked down to the shipyard and located a small rowboat. Thinking there would be no harm in a few hours of use, he commandeered the little craft, slid the oars into place and headed upriver to Johnny Orr's.

The day came and went without Ralph's mother becoming too concerned about his whereabouts, knowing he could have gone off with friends and even had dinner with them. It wasn't until late that night that she raised the alarm.

Residents came out on both the Newcastle and Damariscotta sides of the river and did the best they could in the darkness to no avail. The search resumed the next morning, with large numbers of concerned residents searching miles of shoreline on foot and others searching the river on boats. A small boat was found pushed ashore near Johnny Orr's, with the bowline tied off to a sapling on the riverbank. The underwater scope that Ralph had constructed was found aboard the little craft and had some water in it, as though it had been used. There was no other indication of what had happened to Ralph Mortland, and after several days, the search ended with the presumption that the affable shipwright had been taken by the river.

Mrs. Mortland was beside herself with sorrow. She had already lost her husband, and now she had lost her only son. She faced an old age of loneliness and poverty. She settled into a deep depression that no one could shake her from—until the letter arrived.

The initial circumstances of the letter—mainly the only indication of a return address being the words "Havana, Cuba" on the envelope—had already been known to Everett Dunbar, the reporter who was now furiously taking notes. Now he was to learn the rest of the truth from the woman formerly known as Mary Mortland.

She described opening the letter and watching as dollar bills fell out and floated to the floor. She unfolded the correspondence, and the first words she read were, "Dear Mother." She felt faint and had to take a breath and sit down before she could read the rest of the contents.

Ralph was brief in his explanation. He advised that he was safe and on his way to New York, where he hoped to meet her. He asked her to sell her belongings in Damariscotta and to take the stage to New York as soon as possible. She should go to the Astor Hotel and ask for him, and then he would tell her the complete story.

Mrs. Mortland was in shock. She began weeping, shedding tears of happiness that her son was still alive. After a spell, she regained her composure. She made a decision that, whatever the result, she would follow his instructions and travel to New York. She quietly sold off her possession, and said nothing to her neighbors but good-bye before boarding the southbound stage.

Arriving in New York several days later, she engaged a cabby and went to the Astor. Upon inquiring about her son, a doorman said she had been expected, and she was escorted to an elegant suite and a happy reunification with Ralph. It was then that she learned of her son's adventures after he was last seen rowing upriver in the small boat to Johnny Orr's and disappearing from the village of Damariscotta.

Indeed, using the underwater scope he had constructed, Ralph had been able to position the boat near the rock at Johnny Orr's and survey the river bottom. Sure enough, he saw the partial outline of a chest just under the rock. The tide was slack, so he used the boat's bowline to tie the little craft off on the rock and then he lowered himself from the boat and eased underwater. There it was: a wooden chest with iron bars just like those in his dreams. He returned to the surface and gulped a lung full of air, and then he dove headfirst down to the bottom, where, with some effort, he retrieved the chest from a spot under the rock that had apparently been hollowed out by the tides. After placing the object in his boat, Ralph noticed that the chest was notably heavy and secured with a padlock. Using one of the oars of the boat, he knocked the hinges off the chest, causing the lid to open and spilling a wealth of gold coins into the small vessel.

Still catching his breath from the dive, Ralph was astounded as he watched reflected sunlight dance over the wet surface of the coins. He realized that if somehow his dream were true, there would be two more ironbound chests under the rock. Taking slow, deep and steady breaths in preparation, Ralph sucked in as much air as he could and then dove to the bottom of the river again. When he got down to the underside of the rock, he grasped around in the hollow until he felt another chest and then grabbed it with both hands and pulled it out in a cloud of river silt. Running out of breath, he crouched and placed his feet on the river bottom, using his legs to propel himself up to the surface while holding on to the heavy chest with both arms. Breaking the river surface, he was breathing hard and took a moment to recover his strength before heaving the second chest into the boat.

Ralph was beginning to feel the physical effects of his exertion. His arms and legs felt weak from lack of oxygen, and he was beginning to feel light-headed. He folded his arms over the boat's rail and rested his head on them, trying to build up enough energy for a third dive. He knew that this dive would be the most challenging as the last chest was stuffed farthest back into the hollow. He was hoping that greed wasn't driving him to a watery death, similar to the fate of the pallid man in his dreams.

He rested while the sunlight warmed his shoulders, but he knew that the tide would soon be changing, and that if he was going to make that third dive today, it would have to be soon. He summoned his courage and gathered his strength before taking a last deep breath and plunging back down to the hole under the rock. Underwater, he could feel that the current was running stronger and colder, meaning that the coming tide was bringing cool ocean water up the river. His time at slack low tide had run out.

He found the hollow and stretched his right arm into it, feeling the corner of the third chest with his fingertips. He reached in so far that his face was flush against the mossy surface of the rock. As his hand cast about in the hole for something to grab, he found the padlock on the chest. Grasping it with one hand, he gave a mighty heave, and he could feel the chest move toward him.

Now he was able to get both hands on the padlock and brace his knees against the rock, his lungs starting to burn for lack of air. Finally, the chest came free from the hollow. Holding the chest cradled in his arms with a vise grip, Ralph again pushed off from the bottom and regained the surface.

He gasped for breath as he used the last of his stamina to keep a hold on the chest and not drop it back to the river bottom. He also noticed the current of the incoming tide starting to swirl about him. With a last great heave, he brought the wooden chest over the rail and safely into the boat. Then he clumsily pulled himself over the side and slid down into the boat's interior, breathing heavily as he lay on his back, his face up and feeling the heat of the afternoon sun. He was certain that if he hadn't had the presence of mind to tie his boat up to the rock and instead had to wade back to shore, his strength would have given out, and he would have suffered the same fate as the wraith-like man in his dreams.

But the challenges weren't over yet for Ralph Mortland. Now he had to decide what to do with the treasure. He knew that the local authorities would most certainly impound his newly found wealth until an investigation could be conducted as to where it came from and whom it might belong to. Looking over the gold coins, many of them in foreign denominations, Ralph knew that such an investigation would at best be a long one and at worst end with the authorities permanently confiscating the coins. He decided his best plan would be to remove the coins from any local jurisdiction as quickly as he could and then find a way to convert them to currency.

Ralph slipped the dinghy's bowline from the rock and made his way to the Newcastle shore, where he tied the boat off to a sapling. The area right on the shore of the river was sparsely populated, and he judged correctly that his activities in the river and his landing on shore had gone unnoticed.

He found a thick clump of bushes and hid the chests there. Darkness was just beginning to fall, and there were no signs of alarm that he was missing.

Ralph decided to quietly make his way along the shoreline and through the quiet neighborhoods on Glidden Street so he could reach Jack's Wharf, which he did unnoticed.

Once there, he was lucky enough to find the coasting schooner *Northern Belle* preparing to leave the next morning at first light. He made a deal with the captain and took him into his confidence. The two men then left the schooner and quietly snuck back to Ralph's hiding place in the woods, bringing a small "jigger" (wheeled cart). Loading the treasure into the jigger and covering it with a piece of sailcloth, the two men then walked quietly back through the neighborhoods while most people were at dinner or Sunday worship. The men were able to accomplish this without being seen.

Upon boarding the schooner with his stash, Ralph quickly moved below decks. He remained there when the alarm went out later that night and the initial search was started. Just before sunrise on the Monday morning tide, the little schooner slipped her dock lines and sailed peacefully downriver as worried residents began combing the riverbanks looking for Ralph.

Ralph later explained to his mother how terribly he felt about leaving all those searchers frustrated and his own mother in grief. But he couldn't take a chance on losing what he knew would be a lifetime of comfort for the both of them.

That evening, the schooner sailed past East Boothbay and cleared the mouth of the Damariscotta River. Under full sail with prevailing northeasterly winds, the coasting schooner threaded through the line of offshore islands: first Fisherman's Island to starboard, then Outer Heron to port and finally past Damariscove to the starboard. Then she settled into a southerly course to her destination: Havana, Cuba.

A strong friendship grew between Ralph and the ship's captain, and when they reached Havana, the captain used his local contacts to help Ralph convert the gold into American currency. After sharing a sumptuous dinner with the captain at the best restaurant in Havana, Ralph paid off the captain for his passage and even gave out $100 bonuses to the crew members.

Ralph then headed to the telegraph office to contact his mother but found there was no way to wire a message from Cuba to Maine. He wrote the letter hastily, added some currency for his mother's travel expenses and found a fast packet ship headed for Boston, placing the letter in the care of a messenger service. He then boarded a New York–bound schooner, heading to his final reunion with his mother.

Packed securely in his bags was some $800,000 in currency, which he used to establish his residence at the Astor before settling into an estate on

Fifth Avenue. Later, he carefully invested the money not only in stocks and bonds but also in a variety of his own inventions. The former Mrs. Mortland showed the young reporter a plaque over the fireplace that bore the name of Ralph's new identity, and Dunbar immediately recognized the name as that of a well-known industrialist. It was a secret he knew he would have to keep, but he reckoned that the fantastic story he could reveal was well worth the sacrifice.

When Everett Dunbar bid farewell to the former Mrs. Mortland back in New York City, he knew it would be the last time he would ever see her. He took in the luxurious home and all the elegant furnishings, and he could hardly contain his astonishment that all of this began with a strange dream about a ghostly little man.

Dunbar kept the secret of Ralph and Mary Mortland's new identities for the rest of his life. However, he did document the story of Ralph's discovery at Johnny Orr's and his travels to Havana and finally New York, with the first installment of the series in volume 1, issue 2 of the *Advertiser* in 1876. Residents of the Twin Villages of Damariscotta and Newcastle were relieved to hear that the disappearance of the Mortlands had come to a good end, although there was certainly some grumbling about the two-day search for Ralph. Even so, most true Maine Yankees would sooner fare for themselves with such a find than invite the government to get involved.

Ocean tides still course in and out of the Damariscotta River four times a day, and Johnny Orr's is still a dangerous rapids for any who may want to challenge it on either a coming or going tide.

A key aspect of the legend of Johnny Orr's may still be seen from the shoreline. A lone rock protruding from the tidal flow west of an island located upriver from the Newcastle/Damariscotta Bridge offers the most obvious possibility of Mortland's treasure rock, but its actual location remains uncertain. While in the end, cold hard cash was proof enough of Ralph's recovery of the treasure, what will never be known is if it had been Ralph's dreams alone that took him to that lonely rock, or if perhaps a ghostly pirate had guided his discovery from beyond the dark realm of death.

Chapter 6

THE LADY OF THE HOUSE

The Smith house on High Street in Wiscasset is filled with history, and some say that it is filled with ghosts as well.

Formerly a tavern, the Smith house was later the home of Governor Samuel E. Smith in the 1800s. The white Federal-style house is reportedly haunted by at least three ghosts.

One of the spirits is identified as a Native American named "Seven Days" who used to work at the tavern and still reportedly haunts the landing at the top of a stairway. According to Susan Lowndes Blagden, a sixth-generation Smith descendant who still owns the home, "Seven Days" sleeps at the top of the stairs on a second-floor landing in the house.

Blagden said she watched as her cat tripped over the invisible Native American phantom on the landing. "The cat did a complete somersault, and its hair was standing straight up," according to Bladgen.

"Seven Days" is thought to be a very upset spirit, and it is said that people have heard his voice on the stairway mumbling about a treasure buried in the door-less granite cellar, but no treasure has ever been found.

Another spirit is thought to be "Guy," a dog that belonged to Blagden's great-uncle Samuel, who resided at the house for a time during his later years. Uncle Samuel secluded himself and Guy, a black-and-white setter, into the one-story north wing of the house and lived there for years. Alone in the wing, except for his canine friend, Uncle Samuel pored over his law books, never speaking with family members. The dog would scratch at the door to be let in or out, and people at the house say they can still hear him scratching today.

The house on High Street in Wiscasset occupied by Maine governor Samuel Emerson Smith and his wife, Louisa, in the 1800s. A number of paranormal manifestations have been reported at this historic location, including that of a little old lady who appears in the upper window. She is thought to be the ghost of Louisa. *Photo by Greg Latimer.*

There have also been reports of children's voices coming from the empty attic, as well as footsteps on the stairway when no one is present there.

A woman housesitting at the residence in 1977 had an experience she recalled in the *Wiscasset Newspaper* published in 2002. She found that by confronting the household haunts, she was able to exert some control over them.

She remembered lying in bed in the bedroom at the top of the stairs with a cat next to her and a dog lying on the floor.

"I heard footsteps on the stairway. They were even, measured, and quite heavy," she said. "My immediate thought was that it was the furnace. But at the same time, the dog also [apparently] heard the footsteps and started to whimper.

"The cat, who had been sleeping peacefully, hurriedly climbed under the covers. My heart was literally pounding. I pulled out my best Victorian voice and said, 'We are not amused. Please go away,' and it did."

The woman also recalled a moment when she was in front of the house in the music room.

"I felt like I was being stared at," she said. "I said, 'Excuse me, but I know you don't like me here, but I have a job to do.'"

The woman said that after challenging the spirit, the feeling subsided.

"I think talking with these ghosts helped," she said. "You have to have communication with them."

The long history of this house certainly lends itself to the possibility of multiple hauntings, with perhaps the most intriguing ones being based on a historic occupant of the house: Louisa Sophia Fuller Smith, widow of former Maine governor Samuel E. Smith.

There have been many published reports, all of them different, about when the house was built. However, a plaque located at the building, noting it as a historic location, lists the date as 1801. Other historic records establish that the home was built by Silas Lee, a local attorney who reportedly put the house up for sale when the bank (now the building housing the Wiscasset Library) was built across the street, blocking his view of the harbor. According to an 1899 article in the *Lewiston Evening Journal*, General David Payson purchased the house and then turned it over to his daughter and her husband, "Lt. Page" (neither party clearly identified).

According to the *Evening Journal*, the Page family occupied the house for a number of years before it was purchased by Samuel E. Smith, at the time a judge of the Court of Common Pleas. The exact date of the transaction is not clear, and it was likely that reports that the building was used as a tavern originated sometime during this period as the Smith family and their descendants have owned the building continuously since the initial purchase.

It is known that Judge Smith was elected governor of Maine while he resided at the house and that his term ran from 1831 to 1834. Thereafter, he was reappointed as a judge to the Court of Common Pleas, where he continued to serve until 1837. It is likely that Judge Smith enjoyed the convenience of having his residence located just a one-minute walk away from the Lincoln County Courthouse.

During his time at the residence, Judge Smith raised a family of five sons with his wife, Louisa Sophia Fuller Smith, but the family was continually visited by tragedy.

These tragedies are described in the book *Ghosts That Still Walk*, written in 1941 by Marion Lowndes, a descendant of Judge Smith, who documented the adversity that Louisa Smith endured. Lowndes wrote:

> *It was about a hundred years ago that she lived in the house and raised her family. Through the bitter winters and the unadventurous summers she*

Louisa Sophia Smith, the wife of Samuel Emerson Smith, governor of Maine from 1831 to 1834. This image is taken from a painting at the house on High Street in Wiscasset where the couple resided. It is said that if this portrait and a similar one of her husband are not hung so they are facing each other, they are mysteriously moved to this position. *Image courtesy of the Bladgen family.*

kept house ably and grimly for her husband and the boys. She had no imagination or spirit to soften her life, but she did have endurance. Her youngest son was lost at sea.

Before the Civil War had lasted a year, another son's horse, with stirrups reversed, was following his master's coffin to the graveyard. But she had endurance, and she went on counting her thin silver spoons and scrubbing her white paneled rooms and keeping herself to herself.

Another son died of drink and another became the recluse in the north room and the last one succumbed to pneumonia. Her husband, once able and distinguished, ended his days as a fretful invalid in a wing chair.

"Everything has failed me," Louisa said when she was dying, "except this house. If I can, I'll come back."

It is believed by some family members that Louisa Smith fulfilled her deathbed promise and has, in fact, never left the house, manifesting herself in several compelling ways.

The most intriguing of these stories revolves around a parlor in which the Smiths' possessions were stored after their deaths, including portraits of the couple that hang on the wall. Residents and visitors reported hearing movement in the parlor, as though someone was searching for something within. However, the parlor doors were always locked.

When a curious listener approached the parlor to peek through the keyhole and see what was going on, the noises would suddenly stop.

Finally the residents unlocked the door and entered the room to see for themselves just what was going on. They reportedly noted that some items seemed to have been moved, but it wasn't until they glanced at the portraits hanging on the wall that true shock set in.

Since no one was anticipated to view them in the locked parlor, these portraits had been carelessly hung facing away from each other. Now they were neatly straightened and facing one another.

The parlor was left unlocked, and care was taken that the portraits always faced each other. It was then that sightings of the little old lady reportedly began.

One of the first and most descriptive came from a female visitor to the home who was curiously wandering the hallways one evening. Noticing the parlor door ajar, she opened it to see what was inside. Upon entering, she noticed a little old lady relaxing in a corner chair. The lady seemed content and even friendly. As the visitor stepped toward her to offer a greeting, the little old lady simply smiled and vanished.

Subsequent to this incident, there were various reports, usually having to do with a woman seen in the windows. However, none of these events could be clearly established, save for one.

We heard the story from Susan Blagden, who is Marion Lowndes's daughter.

According to Susan, her parents were visiting New York in the 1950s, when they met a couple from the city. The four became fast friends, and an invitation was extended to the city couple to visit the Wiscasset home should they be traveling to Maine in the future.

Some months later, Susan's parents received a telephone call from the couple advising that they would soon be in the Wiscasset area. Appropriate arrangements were made, but on the day that the couple was expected, some urgent duty arose that the Lowndeses had to attend to immediately.

The front door to the home was left unlocked, and a note left on the kitchen table asking the city couple to make themselves at home.

It should be noted here that the city couple had never been told of any hauntings associated with the home and expected to arrive only to a friendly greeting.

The Lowndeses were gone for several hours and, upon their return, were surprised to find no one at the house. The note appeared to be undisturbed, and it appeared that the house had not even been entered.

They waited the rest of the afternoon, but the city couple never appeared and no phone call was ever received from them. The Lowndeses wondered about the couple's apparent rudeness and then thought no more of it.

Later that year, the Lowndeses were again visiting New York City when they noticed the same couple at a social event. Strangely, the couple seemed distant and angry with the Lowndeses. After some time, the Lowndeses approached them and offered apologies that they had somehow missed their visit. They explained that the front door had been left open, and a note on the kitchen counter had been left inviting them to make themselves comfortable.

Still seeming miffed, the city couple told the Lowndeses that they never got past the front door, saying that they knocked but that "your mother refused to let us in."

The couple went on to describe how their knock at the door had been answered by the appearance of a little old lady in the second-story window. The lady was smiling and seemed friendly, but when the couple knocked again, she just shook her head and refused to answer the door.

Feeling slighted, the city couple left the home with the little old lady still smiling down at them from the window.

Little did they know that no one was home, except perhaps the ghostly Lady of the House.

Chapter 7

A Little Ghost Named Abernathy

The world of make-believe is always part of a household with children, but when make believe turns into a horrifying reality, it can leave things a bit unsettled. Such was the case with a family in Newcastle.

This story begins when a woman we'll call Linda and her husband purchased a farm in north Newcastle in the late 1960s as a summer retreat before moving in year-round in 1973.

The home was historic and well appointed, but the dog (named "Joe Bananas") would refuse to enter the parlor, growling, with the hair on his back standing on end. Linda could find no explanation for the behavior, or any problem with the room, so she simply let Joe Bananas go on about his business, and he continued avoiding any entry into the room.

Linda's family included two children. As many families with children do, they blamed little things that happened around the house (for which no one could be found responsible) on a playful entity. In this case, the family decided to name their entity "Abernathy" and even went on to describe him as a mischievous little boy with flaming red hair.

When one shoe separated from a pair would turn up under a bed, they would say that Abernathy had hidden it. If a faucet was left running and no one 'fessed up, it was another of Abernathy's tricks. If a toy was found left out far from the children's room, it was because Abernathy had been playing with it.

Even if a room felt unusually warm on a cold winter night, the family would laughingly agree it was Abernathy and his flaming red hair.

The farm where the ghost of Abernathy was said to haunt is located near Sheepscot Village. *Photo by Greg Latimer.*

As time went on, these little incidents continued, as they will, and it became a matter of course that Abernathy was always the culprit.

Often in the evenings, Linda would tell the children stories she made up about Abernathy instead of reading them standard bedtime stories. She described the stories as "continual and positive," and they would often end with Abernathy keeping a watchful eye over the children as they slept.

It was almost as though the imaginary Abernathy had become part of the family—imaginary, that is, until Linda was at the Lincoln County Courthouse one day researching old deeds on her property.

There, in the old documents kept on file, she found that the original home on the property had been built in the 1700s by the Woodbridge family. As she continued to read, she found that the home had suffered a tragic fire in which two of the Woodbridge children were killed: a daughter, Sarah; and a son, Abernethy.

While the Woodbridge boy's name was spelled with "e" in the older style, the strange coincidence left Linda in a state of shock.

That shock was soon to take on a new dimension—a photographic one. While remodeling the house, Linda had a photographer come in to take pictures of the progress. Some strange images appeared on the prints.

In each case, Linda said, there was no sign of dust or disturbance in the area when the photos were taken. Likewise, there was no unusual light in the room, and nothing was seen at the time the photos were shot.

However, images appear on the photos that the photographer can't explain, and these images appear to possibly be ghost-like. In one, the outlines of a man and a woman are reported to appear on either side of a fireplace. In another, wispy figures are seen in a corner, two with fairly distinctive "faces."

Aside from these photographs, there was only one other incident where Linda said she might have "seen" Abernathy. It was on a summer day when she and her husband were working in the yard. They happened to glance up to a window in the house and saw the small figure of a boy clad in a white homespun shirt looking down at them. Within seconds, the figure vanished. Upon inspecting the house, no one was inside.

Linda sold the house in 1987 and so ended the family's relationship with Abernathy. But like so many family memories, the photos still remain, and sometimes the bedtime stories are humorously retold at family gatherings.

Chapter 8

HEADLESS GHOST OF DAMARISCOVE ISLAND

Just five nautical miles off the mouth of the Damariscotta River is a small, rocky island that was once home to some of the earliest settlers in the Northeast and what may be Maine's earliest haunting.

It has been home to ghostly sightings and occurrences for over a century, with this reputation mentioned in the 1899 book by John Henry Cartland *Ten Years at Pemaquid: Sketches of Its History and Its Ruins*. Cartland wrote, "Many stories of ghosts, hidden treasures and pirates have been told [of Damariscove]."

The Native American Abenakis were the earliest known residents of the island. The Abenakis called the island "*Aquahega*" or "place of landing." They traveled to the island during the spring months to harvest eggs from the birds nesting there.

As early as 1604, the first European visitors to the island were fishermen who used the island as a fishing station during the summer months. They caught cod, often over six feet long, and dried their catch on racks they built, returning to Europe before winter came to sell their prized dried cod.

Most of their history went unrecorded until the first explorers with navigational skills and logbooks arrived in the late 1500s, finding the fishermen already well established.

While on a mission to explore the Maine coast, Captain George Weymouth anchored off Damariscove in 1605. He returned to England with five captured Native Americans to show off in the king's court while describing the riches of the New World. Various histories describe one of these Native Americans, Squanto, returning to his homeland fluent in English and greeting the Pilgrims when they arrived in Plymouth.

The island's name is attributed to Humphrey Damerill, who was said to have been a member of Popham Colony, some miles south of Damariscove. When that colony failed, Damerill is said to have settled on Damariscove in 1608 to set up a store for the fishermen and a growing island population.

The island was charted with the name "Damerils Iles" by Captain John Smith after a visit in 1614. That name still appeared on charts into the 1700s.

Fishing vessels were being sent to the island on an annual basis from England by Francis Popham, and by 1622, the island had become a year-round residence for thirteen fishermen and two fishing boats. These same fishermen also worked to fortify the island with a wooden palisade and a single mounted gun.

It was also in 1622 that the fishermen of Damariscove helped save the Pilgrims of Plymouth Colony. After a hard winter, the colony was starving to death. In the spring, the colonists sent a boat to Damariscove to plead for

This shack on Damariscove Island may have been used by a past resident and/or visiting fishermen. Presently, it has become a location for the display of lobster trap buoys that float up on the island. The island is home to a headless apparition said to be Richard Pattishall, a sea captain who owned the island in the 1600s and was killed by Native Americans. Pattishall's dog was also killed during the event, and both are said to haunt the island. *Photo by Nicholas Ullo, Boothbay Region Land Trust.*

food. In an act that may have been both kindly and profitable, the fishermen filled the boat with cod.

There were likely trees over most of the eastern half island during these early years, but these were quickly felled by fishermen to build drying racks and later to build the palisades and a few other structures. Within years, the island's rocky surface was completely denuded. The island tree population is only recently starting to return slowly, according to the Boothbay Region Land Trust (BRLT), which presently owns and maintains the island.

In 1672, there were enough year-round inhabitants to petition Massachusetts Bay Colony to create a local government on the island. Damariscove became the first location in Maine to obtain a liquor license allowing a pub established there to serve "beere, wyne and liquors." Perhaps coincidentally, a constable was appointed at about the same time.

Beginning in 1675, the European settlements of New England suffered terribly from a number of conflicts with the Native Americans. In August 1676, a massive Native American assault during King Philip's War was launched on every coastal town near Damariscove. Some three hundred panicked settlers sailed out to the island in a desperate bid for safety. That night, the settlers and island residents watched the dark shoreline across the channel silhouetted by flame as the Native Americans burned every building on the mainland.

The island recovered from the Native American depredations, and by the late 1670s, there were two hundred settlers on Damariscove. A historian later described Damariscove as "the chief maritime port of New England. Here was the rendezvous for English, French, and Dutch ships crossing the Atlantic. Here men bartered with one another and with Indians, drank, gambled, quarreled, and sold indentured servants."

The next Native American conflict was King William's War in 1689. It was during this conflict that the story of the Headless Ghost of Damariscove had its beginnings.

Four years prior in 1685, Captain Richard Pattishall had purchased the island and all of its enterprises. Unknown to him at the time, Pattishall's descendants would include Revolutionary War hero Paul Revere.

In the early months of King William's War, Pattishall and his faithful dog (whose name is lost to time) were in a sloop sailing between Pemaquid and Damariscove when they were attacked by a Native American raiding party.

The attackers succeeded in boarding the craft, killing Pattishall, beheading him and throwing his headless body overboard. Neither records or legend indicate if the head stayed onboard or was also thrown to sea, but it is generally believed that Pattishall's devoted dog jumped overboard, following his master into the depths.

According to local legend, the bodies of both Pattishall and his trusty dog finally washed ashore on Damariscove, and they have been haunting the island ever since.

Through the years, reports of an apparitional headless man and his dog are seen in various locations on the island. Construction workers going about their tasks and Coast Guardsmen standing their watch at the island's lifeboat station reported seeing the ghostly captain and his dog roaming the island. Fishermen in their boats offshore would recall observing the pair in their spectral rounds as they patrolled the shoreline. For some witnesses, the situation was so frightening that they demanded to be taken off the island.

Island caretakers, who stay on the island all summer long, have had mixed experiences with the Pattishall haunt, and other unearthly occurrences on the island.

Nicholas Ullos, presently the executive director of the Boothbay Region Land Trust, the island's current owner, and Tracy Hall spent seven summers on Damariscove as caretakers. According to Tracy, she and Nicholas would pick foggy nights to wander the island in search of the phantom Captain Pattishall and his dog. They never had any success, according to a report in the *Boothbay Register*.

Prior to the Boothbay Region Land Trust's ownership, the island was maintained by the Nature Conservancy, which also stationed caretakers there during the summer months. A reporter for *The Lincoln County News* had an opportunity to interview a pair of these caretakers regarding any paranormal encounters they may have had, and the results were interesting.

The two women both asserted that they had no belief in the paranormal, but one of them was willing to recall a strange experience.

According to the woman, the two caretakers had only recently arrived on the island and were settling in. After a long day, she decided to take a refreshing shower, and in doing so, she removed her wristwatch and set it on a shelf near the shower stall. When she emerged from the shower, her watch was gone. She confronted the other caretaker, thinking that perhaps she was playing a trick on her. However, the caretaker was able to convince her that wasn't the case.

For almost a week, the watch remained missing, until late one night the woman awoke from a sound sleep and found it clasped in her right hand.

"Now I'm not saying a ghost put it there," she said at the time, "but it was pretty strange," she admitted.

The Damariscove Island Museum (right) seen overlooking the inner harbor on the tiny island. The island is administered by the Boothbay Region Land Trust. *Photo by Nicholas Ullo, Boothbay Region Land Trust.*

Another sighting is that of a "Woman in White" who haunts the pond on the east side of the island.

Unusual circumstances at the pond were first reported in the *New England Magazine* in 1895. In an article about Damariscove, Winfield Thompson wrote, "Back of the sheds, about 200 yards away, is a pond, of which many strange tales are told. It is generally described as 'the bottomless pond,' and has alleged to be haunted by a great variety of weird spirits." (The pond is actually estimated to range in depth from four to ten feet.)

Reports of the Lady in White became more frequent after the establishment in 1897 of the United States Life Saving Service Damariscove Station on the southwest part of the island. The Life Saving Service was later replaced by the U.S. Coast Guard. The facility was staffed with crew to man a large rowboat that took to the sea in any kind of weather to rescue sailors from ships that collided with the many shoals near the island.

"People who worked at the Coast Guard station said that they saw a woman in white when they walked from the station to the tower on the other side of the island," according to Tracy Hall. "They said they saw her at night and that she would wave or beckon for them. Some say that she was in the pond and she would try to get them to come into the water."

A view of the Damariscove Island harbor entrance looking out over the open Atlantic Ocean. The Damariscove Lifesaving Station (right) was built in 1897 and was manned until 1959. It was registered in the National Register of Historic Places in 1987 and is now privately owned. *Photo by Nicholas Ullo, Boothbay Region Land Trust.*

One of the Coast Guardsmen was so disturbed by the Lady in White that he requested to be transferred from the island, according to Hall.

Most of the sightings occurred in the 1920s and '30s, while the station was most active, and then declined after the Coast Guard left the station in 1959, according to Hall.

The station is now the only privately owned building on the island. It was entered into the National Register of Historic Places in 1987.

Today, Damariscove is deserted for most of the year, making it impossible to tell what takes place on cold winter nights when the island is buffeted by nor'easter storms. Do the spirits associated with the island dance on the tempestuous winds that come in off the North Atlantic? Or are they fading with time?

Reports persist, especially from those passing the island in boats, of glimpsing a headless apparition walking along the rocky beach. They also report hearing a dog's desperate howl emanating from the shoreline, which is particularly interesting because dogs are not allowed on the island.

Chapter 9

STRANGE HAPPENINGS AT THE RUFUS FLYE HOUSE

E verything seems to change with the passing of time, but a house on Main Street in Damariscotta has actually changed the direction it faces. In spite of the move and constant human activity in and around the building, a group of paranormal entities appears to be undeterred, manifesting in a variety of ways.

Strange mists wander the hallways, heavy footsteps are heard on unoccupied floors and strange images appear on photographs. Perhaps even more frightening: people who work in the building hear a ghostly voice speaking their names.

The potential source for these manifestations is not apparent from the building's historical record. The Federal-style house was built in 1810 for Rufus Flye and in more recent times was the home and office of Dr. Parsons.

In 1984, the original house was lifted off its foundation and turned sideways to allow space for the Damariscotta Bank & Trust driveway. So the front of the present-day building was the western side of the original building. The Mainway Café opened there on the lower floor in 1980 and later became the Salt Bay Café.

Flye was a cabinetmaker and carpenter who was active in both church and civic affairs, including national issues. His participation as a donor was recorded by *Baptist Missionary Magazine* in 1855 and the *African Repository of the American Colonization Society* (a group supporting the freed black slave colony in Liberia) in 1854. He was also a deacon at his church and served as a Damariscotta selectman.

The Rufus Flye house shown on the right before it was lifted and turned ninety degrees. The Vannah Store is shown on the left, and a small gasoline station is in the lot at the end of the driveway. *Photo courtesy of the Damariscotta Historical Society.*

Veterans of the "Grand Old Army of the Republic" (the Union Army during the Civil War) pose for a photograph in front of the Rufus Flye house on Main Street in Damariscotta. *Photo courtesy of the Damariscotta Historical Society.*

His family life was tinged with tragedy, and he lost his daughter Hanna at the age of four and his son, Rufus Jr., at the age of three. Perhaps these early deaths, while not unusual for the period, are one of the reasons for the abundance of paranormal activity at this location.

On the brighter side, records indicate that Flye and his wife, Hannah, did raise three daughters to maturity: Mary, Harriet and Celia. Members of the Rufus Flye family continued to occupy the residence for several generations, with the last being his grandson Rufus Genthner, who resided there in the 1920s.

The most recent residents, who occupied the building into the 1970s before it was converted to offices upstairs with the café downstairs, were Dr. Neil Parsons and his family.

Dr. Parsons was a true rural doctor, keeping an office in his home as well as making house calls. In Maine, house calls included the offshore islands as well. The doctor was often ferried by boat in all kinds of weather to tend to patients injured or ill on these islands, and his hours were always unpredictable.

The present-day Flye House on Main Street in Damariscotta is home to the Damariscotta Region Chamber of Commerce, the Pemaquid Watershed Association and Salt Bay Café. A variety of paranormal activity has been reported by the staff at Salt Bay Cafe, and a number of unexplainable objects have appeared in photos taken near the building. *Photo courtesy of MysteriousDestinationsMagazine.com.*

Dr. Parsons's daughter, Rebecca Parsons, recalled her childhood days at the doctor's house.

"It was a wonderful place to grow up, but it was always busy," Rebecca said. "Patients were coming and going and my father also had office hours in the evening [for people who worked days]."

Rebecca recalls accompanying her father on some of the calls, even traveling offshore with him. "If people called, he had to go," she said.

In 1984, after the Parsons family's residency had ended, the house was lifted and turned to make it more commercially viable, also allowing a driveway to be installed for Damariscotta Bank & Trust next door. Now the building is home to the Salt Bay Café, the Damariscotta Region Chamber of Commerce and the Pemaquid Watershed Association.

Of these three occupants, it is the employees at the Salt Bay Café who spend the most time in the building, especially in the early morning and late-night hours when things are usually quiet.

Soon after the restaurant was purchased by Peter Everett in the late 1990s, he and his staff began having eerie experiences.

The opening cook, who had to arrive early and get things started in the kitchen, kept hearing the hefty door on the west side of the building open slowly and then slam shut, followed by heavy footfalls climbing the stairs and moving through the second floor.

At first, he would leave the kitchen to investigate, but he never found any sign of a surprise visitor. So he started to lock the door, which left him even more mystified when the footsteps continued.

He inspected the door and found that it was still locked and there were no signs of tampering. He glanced around upstairs and found no one and nothing out of place.

Then he started to get just a bit nervous, especially when the door slamming and footsteps continued even when he used an object to block the door. Try as he might, he was never able to actually witness the event.

After some months, he decided he needed the job more than an explanation for the unexplainable door entries and the disembodied footsteps that always followed. Now he considers the noise just another part of the job and doesn't bother to lock the door.

The same door entry and footsteps are sometimes heard by late-night employees as well, although they are more often taken for granted as just another employee in the building.

Strange footsteps in the late night and early morning hours were just the beginning for Peter Everett and his employees at Salt Bay Café. Peter

Salt Bay Café staffers (from left to right) "Peanut" and Peter Everett, both of whom have had paranormal experiences in the building that was formerly the Rufus Flye House in Damariscotta. *Photo by Greg Latimer.*

began seeing vertical mists, some white and some black, crossing through his upstairs office, emanating from one wall and passing through another as they went. A man delivering supplies saw a shadow in the upstairs storage area but could find no source for it. There have also been four occurrences of employees hearing their names used in phrases or whispered in their ears.

In one instance, a waitress helping close the restaurant was busy cleaning in the small kitchen area when she heard someone behind her say distinctly, "I'm right behind you, Wendy." Thinking it was an employee trying to get past her in the narrow confines of the restaurant kitchen, she stepped aside, but no one passed. She immediately looked around and found the kitchen was empty, with no employees present there or in the adjoining dining room.

In another instance, a waitress named Jackie heard her name called and had her hair pulled late at night in the empty dining room.

The other two instances involve a single longtime employee called Peanut. In both cases, she was alone in the dining room straightening tables after a busy lunch shift, and a voice whispered her name in her ear, as though the speaker was right behind her. Upon turning to identify whoever was behind her, she found no one. A quick search of the dining area and a nearby server's station revealed that no one was present.

In Peanut's case, the encounters may have been a warning, perhaps from Dr. Parsons, who passed away in 1983. Shortly after they occurred, she was diagnosed with heart disease and was saved by timely surgery.

Not all employees are able to cope with paranormal visitations as well as these waitresses and the opening cook. A new assistant cook was closing the kitchen one night when he described seeing shadows all around him when the area was empty. He ran out of the building and never returned.

Paranormal manifestations at the Rufus Flye House are not limited to employees at the building. Guests on the Red Cloak Haunted History Tour that stops at the building have captured some strange images on their cameras.

In 2008, a woman photographing the outside of the building where it faces Main Street captured an image that shows a bolt of light radiating from the roof of the building. She hadn't seen the bolt when she took the photo, and she hadn't seen anything that might cause it. The size of the light column was large enough to preclude the possibility that it might be a passing aircraft in the night sky.

In 2011, another woman on the tour was photographing the western side of the building. She saw nothing out of the ordinary while she took a series of photos, but when checking them later, she saw something she couldn't explain. One of the photos in the series had a cluster of bright orange circular objects around the edge of the frame. The exposures before and after the frame showing the unusual objects were unremarkable. According to the woman, there were no lights in the area or droplets of rainfall that may have caused the strange images.

Circular objects, such as those shown in the photo, are sometimes referred to as "orbs" by paranormal investigators. These are discussed in more detail in the chapter found in this book entitled "Haunts and History of the Ancient Burial Ground."

The observations made by the employees and the photos taken during the tours prompted the paranormal exploration team from Damariscotta-based Mysterious Destinations to investigate the building.

The Mysterious Destinations team conducted three late-night explorations of the building, including the Salt Bay Café restaurant as well as the offices of the Damariscotta Region Chamber of Commerce and the Pemaquid Watershed Association.

Participants in an event known as a Midnight Explore at the Rufus Flye House in Damariscotta use a variety of meters to discern the possibility of paranormal activity at the location. *Photo courtesy of MysteriousDestinationsMagazine.com.*

Several unexplained images appeared in photographs, and a weak electronic voice phenomenon (EVP) was recorded. EVPs are digital recordings of voices and other sounds that may have been produced by paranormal sources or activities.

The team also located a number of electromagnetic fields (EMF) in areas where no electricity should have been present. Paranormal investigators believe that such anomalous areas of EMF may indicate paranormal activity.

The investigators are still in the process of evaluating the evidence obtained. When finalized, the results will be published online at MysteriousDestinationsMagazine.com.

In the meantime, employees of and visitors to the businesses at the former Rufus Flye House continue to have unusual experiences, and it's likely that more unexplainable images will be seen in photos taken at the building. Certainly, with hundreds of years of history at the location, there are hundreds of possibilities for what may be causing strange happenings at the Rufus Flye House.

Chapter 10

VISITING MYRTLE

A t a quaint inn located in Newcastle, there is an annual gathering that
includes cocktails, dinner, dessert, an overnight stay and, of course,
breakfast—all of it hosted by the resident ghost.

The "ghostess" hostess is Myrtle Gascoigne, who lived and died in the
building that is now the Tipsy Butler B&B and who owned a nearby antiques
shop that is now the Newcastle Publick House, a popular restaurant. Both
buildings are filled with history as well as Myrtle's haunting presence.

Every year on the Saturday night before Halloween, a small group
(the inn has only four rooms) gathers in the well-appointed sitting room
of the Tipsy Butler to begin an evening of "Visiting Myrtle." The event
starts with a round of introductions while guests enjoy gin and tonic
cocktails, Myrtle's preferred libation. They learn the history of the inn
and Myrtle's association with it, and they are briefed on methods and
equipment used to discern paranormal activity. They dine at the Publick
House and then conduct a paranormal exploration there. They return to
the Tipsy Butler for dessert and another paranormal exploration before
settling down in their rooms. Some sleep well through the night. Others
continue to visit—sometimes on their terms, sometimes on Myrtle's.

Further details of the paranormal activity attributed to Myrtle during the
annual event will be discussed later. First we'll introduce the reader to Myrtle
and the history of her home and hauntings.

Myrtle was a strong, assertive woman with an outgoing personality in
life, and she continues to be even after her death in 1980 at age eighty, on

The Tipsy Butler B&B in Newcastle, the former (and perhaps current) residence of Myrtle Gascoigne. *Photo by Greg Latimer.*

November 1, All Hallows Day. That may explain why her spirit seems so active during the Visiting Myrtle event held during the last Saturday of October. Many of her manifestations at both the Tipsy Butler and the Publick House appear to be efforts on her part to assert her will or communicate concerns about the buildings she was so personally invested in.

Well before the current owners of the Tipsy Butler arrived, the former owners were in the process of remodeling some of the rooms at the inn. As one owner discussed changing the paint colors in an upstairs bedroom, a brush suddenly and forcefully flew from a stationary position on a dresser directly at her head. She had to duck quickly to avoid injury. Needless to say, the paint color remained the same.

While Myrtle enjoyed the occasional gin and tonic, she was also known to be adamant against the excessive consumption of alcohol. Because of this personality trait, the owners of the Publick House blame one interesting incident entirely on Myrtle. One busy night, the sound of hundreds of bottles crashing to the floor of the downstairs storage area alarmed both staff and guests at the Publick House.

Management personnel ran downstairs worried that someone may have been injured in whatever accident had occurred, but no staff member was present. Instead, they found that a large shelf made of solid steel containing all of their liquor bottles had somehow fallen forward, breaking most of the

Above: The parlor at the Tipsy Butler B&B in Newcastle where one guest described a woman who directed him to the ice machine. However, except for that guest, the inn was empty at the time. *Photo by Greg Latimer.*

Right: Myrtle Gascoigne at age nineteen. *Photo courtesy of the Tipsy Butler B&B.*

contents. The shelf had stood in the same location for years, with employees stocking and restocking it. No one had ever seen it so much as wobble, much less appear to be unsteady in any way. The restaurant owners could only shake their heads and chide Myrtle for causing such a loss, believing that her feelings about immoderate alcohol consumption had caused her to somehow topple the shelves.

Fortunately, Myrtle's manifestations are not always so violent or dramatic. She can also be helpful.

On one such occasion, the Tipsy Butler was hosting a wedding party. Both the guests and the inn's staff were at a nearby restaurant, when a member of the party, running late, arrived at the inn. Following directions on a note left by the innkeeper, he went upstairs to his room to deposit his luggage and then returned downstairs to locate the ice machine, which the note described as being in the dining room. While glancing around in an effort to find the machine, he saw a woman standing in the sitting room just outside the door

The Newcastle Publick House in Newcastle, formerly an antique ship owned by Myrtle Gascoigne, whose spirit is said to continue to haunt the location. *Photo by Greg Latimer.*

to what was once Myrtle's bedroom and asked her if she knew where the dining room was. She simply pointed toward the adjoining dining room, and he followed her direction, turning a corner to find the ice machine. After retrieving a bucketful of ice, the guest returned back through the sitting room, expecting to find the woman there so he could thank her. He was disappointed but not too surprised when he didn't see her, assuming she had returned to her room, so he returned to his.

Later, when the rest of the wedding party returned, he learned that all the inn's guest and staff had been at the restaurant and that the building should have been entirely empty except for him. The innkeepers smiled and advised the guest that he had just met Myrtle, and then everyone thanked her for helping out.

In another case of Myrtle's penchant for lending a ghostly hand, paranormal explorers during the 2012 Visiting Myrtle event began to notice a certain trend to some responses they were getting via their equipment. Myrtle seemed concerned about the condition of the building housing the inn. Using instruments such as electromagnetic field detectors, dousing rods,

The Butler's Room at the Tipsy Butler B&B in Newcastle where Myrtle Gascoigne died. This room is always full of paranormal activity during the annual Visiting Myrtle event at the inn. *Photo by Greg Latimer.*

pendulums and even flashlights, the guests at Visiting Myrtle could pose "yes" or "no" questions and wait for Myrtle's response using one of the instruments. (Digital voice recorders were also used to discern electronic voice phenomena, called EVP, but there were no discernable EVPs found on this occasion.)

Through a series of questions, the guests were able to determine that Myrtle was concerned about the chimney and possible damage from water that might occur during the winter months. The innkeepers were advised, but despite their efforts to ascertain where a problem could develop, there was a water leak in the furnace, which is located near the chimney base, that caused considerable damage to the inn that winter.

For Tipsy Butler innkeeper Sarah Davison-Jenkins, Myrtle's effort to communicate a problem with the building's condition is just another aspect of the day-to-day relationship she maintains with the spirit.

"Myrtle is definitely part of the management team here—in fact, she may actually be the one in charge," Sarah said. "I'm constantly either asking for her advice or watching to see how she responds to changes."

Sarah admits that during the day she often has "conversations" with Myrtle as she goes about her tasks. "I'm never lonely, and I hope Myrtle isn't either," Sarah said.

Sarah Davison-Jenkins, innkeeper at the Tipsy Butler B&B in Newcastle. Davison-Jenkins maintains a relationship with her resident ghost and good friend Myrtle Gascoigne. *Photo by Greg Latimer.*

Born Myrtle Sage in New Jersey circa 1900 or 1901, at the age of nineteen, Myrtle married George Gascoigne, a successful lawyer with interests in insurance and banking, who resided in the New York area.

Her first child, Nancy, arrived circa 1926, and it was just before or after this time that Myrtle decided to move out of the New York area and into the sparsely populated countryside as a way of avoiding polio infections in her children.

All but eradicated in modern times, polio was a dreaded disease primarily infecting infants and children until a vaccine was developed in the 1950s. The youthful victims of this horrifying disease were often left completely or partially paralyzed, and in some cases, this paralysis affected the lungs, forcing the patient to survive using a large chamber called an "iron lung." Technically, the device was known as a "negative pressure ventilator" that would use changes in air pressure within the chamber fifteen times a minute to cause the patient's rib cage to expand and contract, causing them to "breathe." While a lifesaver, the device was also a virtual prison from which the patient could not escape until the polio developed into another stage or the patient died. Fortunately, this device was usually only required for several weeks during the initial stages of the disease when lung paralysis was most prevalent. However, in some cases, the treatment period could last for decades.

Martha Ann Lillard of Oklahoma was placed in an iron lung because of polio paralysis in 1953 and, due to the fact that she is not a good a candidate for portable respirators, still remains hospitalized in an iron lung to this day. Some six to eight other patients in the United States share her fate, according to a report on NBC television.

New York suffered from a severe polio epidemic in 1916, with nine thousand cases reported and 25 percent of them ending in fatalities. Memories of this epidemic must have still been vivid when Myrtle's first child was born. Not much was known then about how polio spread, but it was clearly quite contagious, and presumably with her husband's approval, Myrtle headed north to Maine.

In Newcastle, she found a home that had possibly been used as a boardinghouse, based on its proximity to the railroad station, or may have been a multi-bedroom residence. It was located on what was then Cross Street (now High Street) and had a beautiful view of the Damariscotta River and the Twin Villages of Newcastle and Damariscotta. Based on a combination of anecdotal history from Myrtle's surviving family members and town records, Sarah believes that Myrtle's husband purchased the home along with several other structures and property nearby, an area that comprises the length of present-day High Street. He then "gifted" or otherwise transferred ownership of the property to Myrtle.

It was a rare thing in the early 1900s for a woman to own such a fine property, and it must have been a great source of pride for Myrtle. Sarah suspects that Myrtle's sense of pride and achievement continues to this day.

While Myrtle continued to maintain an official address with her husband in the New York area, she and the children spent much of their time at the home in Maine. A 1940 census shows the family—including Myrtle at age thirty-nine; her husband, George Gascoigne, at age forty-four; and her children: Nancy, nineteen; Sally, fifteen; and Robert, thirteen—all living in Rye, Westchester County, New York.

Subsequent to this census, George Gascoigne passed away, and Myrtle married George Schroeder. However, she continued to keep her primary residence at her home in Newcastle.

At some point, Myrtle either acquired or rented the former Glidden-Austin block building located at the intersection of Academy Hill and Business Route 1 in Newcastle, a short walk away from her home. She established an antique and collectible items store there, where she was featured in the June 1968 edition of *National Geographic* as part of an article entitled "Character Marks the Coast of Maine." She continued to operate the store until shortly before her death. That building is now the Newcastle Publick House.

Several stories passed down through family members over the years offer some insight into the colorful character of Myrtle. She was known as an avid opponent of alcohol use, but there were some exceptions. In 1875, a distillery in Poland Spring, Maine, created a unique liquor bottle for the grand opening of the Poland Spring Hotel. The bottles were molded to create a likeness of the biblical figure Moses and hence named "Moses Bottles." They were filled with gin, sloe gin and whiskey, and while they came into general circulation in Maine, they were considered collectible by those visiting from "away" (as Mainers refer to the area outside of their state). Between the first Moses Bottle in 1875 through the final version in 1972, forty-three varieties of Moses Bottles were created, some now valued as high as $200.

According to family members, Myrtle enjoyed the Moses Bottles filled with gin. She would use the gin to mix up a refreshing gin and tonic (or two) for herself, and then she would sell the empty bottles in her store. Moses Bottles are still used at the Tipsy Butler as "trigger devices" to catch Myrtle's attention during the annual Visiting Myrtle paranormal event at the inn, as are copies of the *National Geographic* (mentioned above) with a full-page photo of Myrtle comfortably ensconced in her store surrounded by shelves full of unique items. She is nattily clad in a Hawaiian-print shirt and a straw hat that could best be described with the modern-day term "funky." She is apparently gesticulating to the photographer while in conversation and is described in the caption as "elbow deep in antiques."

Another quirky habit of Myrtle's was the use of her children as store detectives for her antique shop. According to family members, she would assign the children to follow certain suspicious customers through the store to ensure that they paid for what they plucked from her shelves.

Myrtle's past involvement with the building that is now the Newcastle Publick House is likely why her spirit is still active at the location, according to Sally Lobkowicz, the director of Mysterious Destinations, a Damariscotta-based tour company that conducts the Visiting Myrtle event.

"The strength of Myrtle's personality in life, and the personal investment she had in both the Newcastle Publick House and Tipsy Butler buildings, has apparently given her the capability to haunt both locations," Lobkowicz said. In fact, Myrtle may also have the ability to move back and forth between the two locations at will, sometimes apparently following guests as they walk to and from the Publick House during the Visiting Myrtle event.

"On two occasions, our EMF detectors have registered a strong field that moves right along with guests as they travel between the buildings," Lobkowicz said. "We have even tried changing sides of the street to eliminate any possible interference from overhead wires, and the field continues with us at the same strength."

Like Sarah at the Tipsy Butler, most employees at the Publick House accept Myrtle's presence as part of their working environment—except in rare cases. Such a case occurred with a new employee who was unfamiliar with Myrtle. Sent on a task into the basement storage area one night, she returned visibly shaken. Other employees tried to comfort her and find out what had transpired, but she never revealed what had happened to her and refused to go down to the basement ever again.

Some employees also report a feeling of dread or that of being watched in the basement area. These types of negative experiences are very rare for those encountering Myrtle, and Lobkowicz attributes them to the possibility that there may be more than one haunting at the Publick House.

"This is a building with a history that long predates Myrtle; it was built in 1845 and served as the federal customs house among other things," Lobkowicz said. "That would explain why some folks have had paranormal experiences here inconsistent with the usual experience we have with Myrtle."

Records indicate that the building was known as the Glidden-Austin block and was used as a ship's chandlery and tenement housing in its early years. The building is also known as the "Customs House." However, no historical record (including that of the Library of Congress) could confirm that it was ever used in this function. Perhaps the services of the ship's chandlery included customs inspection, as the closest U.S. customs houses were over ten miles away in Waldoboro to north and Wiscasset to the south. Federal sources also indicate that the building included a funeral home at some point. In 1854, it was the first location for the Newcastle State Bank, which became Newcastle National Bank during the Civil War. In later years, during a Depression-driven bank holiday declared by President Franklin Roosevelt, the First National Bank of Damariscotta merged with the Newcastle National Bank and is still doing business in Damariscotta as The First, N.A. In any case, there were certainly many opportunities for the building to attract restless spirits in the years before Myrtle's rambunctious presence made an entrance.

The dining room at the Newcastle Publick House in Newcastle, where employees have several times reported seeing the apparitional image of a woman thought to be Myrtle Gascoigne. *Photo by Greg Latimer.*

Some incidents at the Publick House (as well as those previously mentioned) bear Myrtle's signature style, in spite of what might be a ghostly overpopulation at the building.

Two of these are full-bodied apparitions—the type that makes the observer believe he or she is actually seeing a person—like the incident mentioned previously at the Tipsy Butler with a wedding guest.

Both incidents occurred late at night when the main lights were darkened and only a small number of employees were engaged in the final tasks of the night. Both incidents involved an employee glimpsing a person in the dining room area, and both times, the employees assumed the person was a fellow employee. Of course, they would soon discover that no employees were in the area at the time of the sightings.

The incidents at Tipsy Butler during the Visiting Myrtle event began very slowly and then increased to the point that over thirty-six minutes of videotape showing Myrtle responding to questions through a variety of devices was obtained during the 2012 event.

The first Visiting Myrtle event was relatively quiet, as though Myrtle was both cautious and curious about her houseguests and their activities. Responses on various devices were minimal and inconclusive until the guests settled down for the night.

All of the guests were provided with trigger devices, including a Moses Bottle and a copy of the *National Geographic* magazine that featured Myrtle. They were also provided with an EMF detector to keep on their nightstands. The EMF detectors have a flashing red light that signals the presence of an EMF and an optional audible alarm that makes a loud beeping sound when the volume is turned up.

One couple sleeping in the upstairs "Groundskeeper's Room" had the volume up and was rudely awakened when the detector activated loudly at

Shown in this photo taken during a Midnight Explore at the Tipsy Butler B&B in Newcastle are some of the devices used to discern the presence of paranormal activity. *From left to right*: an adjustable flashlight, as flashlights are sometimes turned on or off by an unknown presence; a "Mel" meter designed especially to monitor a variety of atmospheric conditions; and an electromagnetic field (EMF) detector designed specifically to discern electromagnetic activity that may indicate a paranormal presence. (Note: The EMF detector is metering a field as indicated by the needle near the halfway mark on the gauge.) *Photo by Greg Latimer.*

about 2:00 a.m. As soon as they could identify the source of the disturbance and try to grab a camera to photograph it, the EMF apparently moved away and the detector response subsided. A nearly identical incident occurred again at 4:00 a.m.

Most paranormal experts agree that an EMF found where it shouldn't be indicates the potential for a paranormal presence. Certainly, an EMF that seems to move about on its own, and apparently in response to human interaction, creates a strong possibility of a paranormal presence.

In the years following the first event, Myrtle seemed to be waiting all year for her annual guests. Various incidents begin occurring with the first arrivals and continue into the night, with Myrtle manifesting on a variety of devices.

"We definitely get the feeling that Myrtle is welcoming us and that she wants to communicate with us," Lobkowicz said. "We always thank her for welcoming us back!"

As for the rest of the year, Myrtle and Sarah make their daily rounds at the Tipsy Butler, freshening rooms and preparing meals, always keeping the inn ready for visitors and up to Myrtle's very specific qualifications.

Chapter 11

HAUNTS AND HISTORY OF THE ANCIENT BURIAL GROUND

In a quiet neighborhood several blocks north of the bustling traffic on U.S. Route 1 in Wiscasset is a cemetery that dates back to 1739.

Aged headstones at the Ancient Burial Ground on Federal Street bear silent testimony to the triumphs and tragedies that visited Wiscasset during the early years of settlement there. Many more grave markers, made of wood instead of stone, have fallen victim to the elements and are no longer visible, leaving the names of those interred beneath them lost in a historical void.

In more recent times, the picture-book cemetery has been the location for several reports of paranormal activity. Since paranormal activity is often associated with the bygone times of a location, we'll first examine the history and funerary culture associated with the Ancient Burial Ground.

The oldest known marker at the site is that of Joshua Poole, who died in 1739 when the canoe he was in capsized, leaving both Poole and his brother-in-law Samuel Tarr to drown in the cold, swift waters of the Sheepscot River. Poole's body was recovered, but Tarr's was not. It is unknown if there was any type of memorial set in place by Tarr's family, but Poole's memorial can be located in the southeast quadrant of the cemetery to the right of the entrance on Lincoln Street after walking about sixty feet into the cemetery under a tree to the east (toward the river). The simple marker is a slate stone with a skull.

There are two stories about how the men came to their demise, both of them anecdotal. The most common version involves a bear attacking the canoe in shallow water, with the men tossed helplessly into the river. The other version is not quite as dramatic, with a rope parting as the men were pulling the anchor up, causing the canoe to capsize with the sudden shift of weight. Either version would have had a predetermined ending for the men. Like many others of their day, neither Poole nor Tarr could swim a single stroke, so their fate was cast the second they found themselves overboard.

Poole was thirty-nine years old when he died, leaving his wife, Deliverance, who was pregnant at the time, and two children. Only one of the children, a son, lived long enough to marry, according to records.

The community re-cut and reset Poole's stone in 1866 "out of respect for its age and the circumstances under which Joshua died," so modern-day visitors to the grave may be disappointed they're not seeing the original 1739 marker. These visitors shouldn't worry for long, for a quick look around will reveal many markers bearing dates in the 1700s and 1800s, all with their own stories.

The Ancient Burial Ground has several graves of Revolutionary War veterans. One of the more prominent of these Revolutionary War figures is Ezekiel Averil, who was in General George Washington's personal guard. The compilation *Massachusetts Soldiers and Sailors of the Revolutionary War* (Maine was still part of Massachusetts at that time), published in 1896, listed Averil as a private in Captain Mill's company, part of Colonel Jeduthan Baldwin's Regiment of "artificers," an archaic term that describes soldiers who had particular skills. In modern military terminology, they would be somewhat like "specialists."

It is likely that Averil's "artifice" was as a musician, since a subsequent enlistment during the War of 1812 listed him as such.

While it may be hard to understand why George Washington's personal guard required musicians, it becomes clearer when the entire unit is examined. Created in 1776 and officially known as the Commander in Chief's Guard, the unit was charged with protecting George Washington and important papers related to the Continental army. To ensure complete representation in protecting the general, and because service in the unit was considered an honor, the ranks of the Chief's Guard included members from each of the original thirteen colonies. They were with General Washington at every battle and attached to his headquarters.

In a 1904 history, *The Commander-in-Chief's Guard*, author Carlos Godfrey provided details regarding the unit, including a complement of six drummers, six fifers and a drum major. This selection of musicians would have been used to set the rhythm for a steady march, but they would have figured into any action fought as well.

Averil's headstone is a well-worn white marker located in the northwest quadrant of the cemetery, somewhat close to Federal Street.

There are numerous other grave sites for veterans and victims of historic wars. One pair is particularly moving: the plain white headstones of two brothers lost in the Civil War.

The stones are located in the southwest corner, just a short distance from the fence corner at Federal and Lincoln Streets: one bearing the name of Sidney O. Kingsbury, Company F, Second Maine Cavalry, who passed on September 20, 1864; and the other bearing the name of John H. Kingsbury, Company Q, Fourth Maine Infantry, who died just a month later on October 24, 1864.

Nothing could be found in the records about the service of Sidney Kingsbury, but records of his cavalry regiment show it was assigned to the "Dept. of the Gulf," the southern states of Louisiana, Mississippi, Alabama and Florida.

Only 2 officers and 8 enlisted men from the cavalry regiment were killed outright on the battlefield or mortally wounded. However, 334 enlisted men

A view of the Ancient Burial Ground in Wiscasset, a location with grave markers that date back to the 1700s. The two stones in the right foreground are of Civil War casualties, brothers John H. Kingsbury of the Fourth Maine Infantry (left) and Sidney O. Kingsbury of the Second Maine Cavalry. *Photo by Greg Latimer.*

died of disease for a total 344 fatalities. With these figures, combined with his date of death, it would seem likely that Sidney succumbed to disease during an expedition from Barrancas to Marianna in Florida that the cavalry undertook from September 18 to October 4, 1864.

The record on John Kingsbury confirms his service in the Fourth Maine Infantry, which was mustered in Rockland in 1861 and marched south to join the Army of the Potomac. Initially, the untried unit was thrown into the defense of Washington, D.C. Shortly thereafter, the soldiers fought their first major action, surviving the crucible of fire during the Battle of Bull Run on July 21, 1861 (known as Manassas on the Confederate side).

The Fourth Maine was to continue taking casualties for the next three years, fighting on a number of battlefields, including the Second Bull Run, the Battle of Fredericksburg, the Battle of Gettysburg and the Battle of the Wilderness. The regiment lost 14 officers and 156 enlisted men to battlefield action, as well as 2 officers and 185 enlisted men to disease, for total of 307 fatalities.

The Fourth Maine Infantry was mustered out on July 19, 1864, at which time veterans and recruits transferred to the Nineteenth Maine Infantry. This timing leaves us with a bit of mystery about what John's situation was at the time of his death in October 1864, which was after the regiment's term of service had ended. It could be that he died of wounds or disease that had occurred during the regiment's active duty or that he had been taken prisoner and died while in custody. Either way, it's certainly an unfortunate circumstance that John perished after surviving so many horrific and bloody battles.

Located right at the entrance of the Ancient Burial Ground is a very unusual cemetery piece called a table marker or table tomb. These were popular for a short period of time in the 1830s, although there's nothing in the record that indicates why.

This marker memorializes three of William and Eliza Stacey's children: Silas, Nancy and Mary Eliza, who met untimely deaths at early ages between May and June 1833. Also included is memorial script for a one-year-old daughter who had passed away previously in 1830. There is no mention on the stone, or in existing public records, of what caused the deaths of the three children in such a short period of time. However, epidemics of disease were common during the period.

Wiscasset residents suffered terribly during the spotted fever (smallpox) epidemic of 1814. The epidemic is mentioned in the book *Trail of the Maine Pioneer Women* in an article by Maude Clark Gay, who writes that the town

Above: This unusual cemetery piece found in the Ancient Burial Ground is called a table marker or table tomb. These were in vogue during the 1830s. The large surface of these markers allowed relatives to leave long inscriptions and to mark multiple graves. Four members of the same family, all children, are memorialized by this marker. *Photo by Greg Latimer.*

Left: This headstone gives testimony to the seafaring life that many residents of Maine depended on for a living and how deadly this living could be. The two names on the lower part of the stone were both seafarers who never returned home. One was "lost at sea," and very possibly that is all that was known of his demise at age twenty-six. The second "died in Matanza, Cuba," quite probably of disease, at age thirty-five. It is unlikely that the bodies of these men ever returned to home port, and the hallowed ground under this headstone is probably not their final resting place. *Photo by Greg Latimer.*

"fell a victim to the terrible fever plague, which claimed as its prey so many prominent citizens of Wiscasset. During its prevalence nearly every store in the town was closed, and it is related that for over a month a vapor or deep fog obscured the sun here, although it shone brightly in the adjoining towns. Night after night blazing tar barrels disinfected the air, and the specter of death and despair spread its ghostly arms over the fair village."

Many early Wiscasset residents relied on a living from the sea, either as fishermen or blue water sailors. Such a lifestyle was fraught with danger and still is today.

One of many headstones at the Ancient Burial Ground that give testimony to the hazards of seafaring life can be found in the southwestern quadrant of the cemetery, near the headstones of the Kingsbury brothers.

The headstone records two tragic deaths of Wiscasset sailors, J.C. Felker Jr. and William C. Felker. The untimely death of eleven-year-old John C. Felker is also recorded on this stone.

The younger Felker, who passed away in 1821, probably died in town based on his age and the fact that no location is mentioned.

J.C. Felker Jr. is remembered as many sailors have been: "died at sea." His date of death at the relatively young age of twenty-six is listed as September 17, 1835. No location or cause is given, and it is likely these are lost in time.

William C. Felker "died in Matanza, [actually Matanzas] Cuba," in 1852 at age thirty-five. Immediately preceding the Civil War, trade with Maine and Cuba was vigorous. Matanzas was a bustling port in the northwestern part of Cuba and home to many sugar cane plantations. With a slave population estimated at over 100,000 in an 1859 census, Matanzas was also the site of several slave insurrections during the time period Felker may have been active there. However, it is most likely that Felker fell victim to a mosquito-borne disease. Three rivers flow into the bay where the city located, providing plenty of slow-moving water in delta areas nearby.

It is unlikely that the bodies of the two sailors were ever returned to home port, and the hallowed ground under this headstone is probably not their final resting place. Likewise, given the span of years recorded on the headstone, it would appear the Felker family may have been trying to memorialize these three members more affordably by including them all on one headstone, so we may never know if the body of young John C. Felker resides at this spot as well.

Aside from the paranormal incidents soon to be discussed, the Ancient Burial Ground offers the visitor a virtual museum of period funerary markers. A pleasant summer afternoon can be spent examining the headstones, admiring the artwork and learning more about all of the small personal stories that collectively become what we refer to as "history."

As with many cemeteries, the Ancient Burial Ground has been the site of strange occurrences. People walking by the area at night sometimes see shadowy movements or strange lights. Others hear voices on the wind. One woman described holding a séance in an effort to connect the ghosts of a mother and her baby. She described being brought to tears by the experience, followed by a feeling of extreme calm.

Perhaps the most compelling incidents come from guests on the Red Cloak Haunted History Tours that make regular visits to the Ancient Burial Ground in the early evening hours, always staying on the sidewalk beyond the fence out of respect for those interred at the cemetery.

There have been two sightings by guests of these tours, both in the southwest quadrant where the previously discussed Kingsbury and Felker headstones are located.

The first of these involves an ethereal mist that appeared in a photograph taken at the location, despite that fact that environmental conditions were not conducive to mists or fog.

The mist reveals a figure that appears to be wearing a cloak, rising up from the ground between some headstones. While such an image is subjective to interpretation, many people who see the photo are able to discern a face with hollow eye sockets staring out from under the cloak hood.

Left: The urn and the willow were very common markings on headstones of the 1800s. The willow symbolized mourning, and the urn symbolized death. The purpose of the two "Xs" on this stone is lost in time. *Photo by Greg Latimer.*

Right: The marking on this headstone is called a cherub, which was a popular symbol in the 1800s. *Photo by Greg Latimer.*

Another photo, taken by a seventeen-year-old girl visiting from Texas, is even more compelling. It reveals two circular objects among the headstones, both clearly defined and with concentric circles emanating from their centers. They were seen in the photograph but not by the photographer. She noticed them only minutes after she took the photo, while she was checking the small screen on the back of her camera. "I didn't really want to tell anyone at first," she said at the time. "I just couldn't believe they were there."

In this particular case, an experienced photographer was with the group. He was able to establish that the cold, clear evening was free of precipitation, dust particles or insects. He was also able to transfer the image from the girl's camera almost immediately to a laptop computer, thereby precluding any possibility that there was a chance to "enhance" the image.

The photographer also checked the camera for any malfunctions and checked to see if any other unusual images from the cemetery were present on the camera.

The type of objects photographed that night at the Ancient Burial Ground are called "orbs" by paranormal investigators, and they are controversial because they can be caused by a number of things, not all of them from the paranormal realm.

Officially, researchers define orbs as "photographic anomalies" (something appearing in the photograph that has no technical or environmental explanation). Nonetheless, these "anomalies" can be quite interesting, appearing in a variety of sizes and patterns. There are many versions of orbs, and they are usually seen in digital photographs. There is plenty of speculation about them.

Water droplets and even dust motes can appear as orb-like objects in digital photos because the digital camera has an extensive field of focus that causes small things near the camera that we can't "see" with our eyes to appear as huge things in the image due to their closeness to the lens. Atmospheric, lighting and other conditions must be examined to determine if orb images can be logically explained. When no explanations are found, the images are considered anomalies.

In contrast to the beliefs of skeptics about orbs, paranormal researchers believe that orbs are disembodied spirits—in other words, ghosts. There are claims that human faces can be seen in some orbs and that orbs emit electromagnetic energy.

Anyone using an Internet search engine to check the word "orbs" will find a considerable amount of conflicting information on the subject. But some tests are still lacking.

"No one has ever put a dust mote in a vacuum and photographed it with a digital camera so that we can actually see what a dust mote looks like when photographed digitally," said one paranormal researcher. "Instead, you'll have an image of an orb in a scientifically uncontrolled environment, with one expert telling you it's a dust mote and another one telling you it's their late Uncle Charlie. That's why we prefer to investigate logical explanations, and then—if none can be found—we label the image an anomaly."

According to Sally Lobkowicz, director of Red Cloak Haunted History Tours, that type of process is consistent with her own theme for the tours. "People often ask us if we believe in ghosts, and our response is that we believe in anomalies."

Anomalies or ghosts? It is still unknown what exactly is happening at the cemetery, but with so much history at the location, the possibility that a visitor might photograph a disembodied spirit is just another reason to visit the Ancient Burial Ground of Wiscasset.

Chapter 12

HAUNTED COLONIAL PEMAQUID

Most paranormal experts agree that spirits seem drawn to locations with geography, structures and artifacts that were part of their earthly existence. Such objects and areas are called "triggers" because they tend to trigger a response in the paranormal entities.

Perhaps the largest, most complete and most accurate trigger in the Damariscotta area is the Colonial Pemaquid historic site on the Bristol peninsula. With a museum full of artifacts, a fort rebuilt to historically accurate specifications, a cemetery dating back to the first settlers, a fort house built in the 1700s and a field full of cellar foundations dating back to the 1600s, if Colonial Pemaquid isn't haunted, it probably should be—and some say it is.

The Colonial Pemaquid State Historic Site is one of the earliest sites of European occupation in North America. It was used as a seasonal fishing station as early as 1610 and was the location of a permanent village settled between 1625 and 1629.

In 1677, Fort Charles, the first of three forts on the site was built. Extensive archaeological excavations have unearthed fourteen foundations of seventeenth- and eighteenth-century structures and the officers' quarters for Fort William Henry and Fort Frederick. A museum displays hundreds of artifacts found on the site, dating from prehistoric times through the colonial period. Musket balls, coins, pottery and early hardware are among items of interest.

The site includes an early twentieth-century reconstruction of Fort William Henry housing a permanent exhibit titled "Guns, Politics and Furs."

This replica of Fort William Henry, located at Colonial Pemaquid, offers visitors a chance to climb up into the parapets and see the area from the same angle as the colonists who originally populated the site. A Native American captive is said to have died at the location, and some observers have attributed a misty presence that floats in the fort area to his tortured spirit. *Photo by Greg Latimer.*

These foundations built by some of the nation's earliest European settlers at Colonial Pemaquid overlook the scenic Pemaquid Harbor. *Photo by Greg Latimer.*

This replica of a seventeenth-century house at Colonial Pemaquid gives visitors an idea of what the structures built on the foundations still visible on the site looked like. The structure is built around a post-and-beam frame, and then wattle and daub was added, a process that refers to a building technique that has been in use for over one thousand years. The process describes a system of filling in the walls of the framework of a house, usually wood, with a mixture of mud, sand, crushed rock, lime, chopped straw and any similar materials that were available to the colonial builders. This mixture—the "daub"—is thoroughly blended, formerly by feet, both human and animal. It is then plastered onto a mesh framework of vertical and horizontal strips of wood or saplings. This is the "wattle." It took considerable effort on the part of a volunteer team to construct this building, which will remain on display and continue to be improved. There are examples of this ancient method of construction all over the world. In Europe, many such homes are hundreds of years old and still in use. *Photo by Greg Latimer.*

In addition to the historic buildings and sites in the park, there is spectacular scenery and a picnic area that make Colonial Pemaquid a great destination not just for history buffs but also for those just looking to enjoy a day on the Maine shoreline.

One of the frequently reported sightings is that of an ethereal mist that takes on a vertical shape and is seen drifting from the fort to a tree close the shore. Some believe that the apparition is the spirit of a Native American who, after arriving at the fort peacefully to negotiate a treaty, was instead imprisoned and chained to a large rock that can still be seen inside the fort. It is said that during his captivity, the only time he was allowed to leave the confines of the stone redoubt was to be led by a chain on his wrists down to the tree.

It's unknown if it was the captivity that caused him to lose his will to live, but it is known that he eventually died in the confines of his prison, still chained to the rock.

Observers believe that his ghost still walks the lonely path between the fort and the tree. Dusk and dawn have been described as the best times to see the evanescent mist.

There have also been reports and some paranormal explorations of the Fort House. The spirit of a child may have been present, objects were moved on shelves and footsteps were heard coming to the door of a room and stopping there, according to a source familiar with the exploration.

On one occasion, in full daylight, a visitor just outside the fort, near where foundations of troop quarters can still be seen, saw the full-bodied apparition

The Fort House at Colonial Pemaquid was built in the late 1700s. It presently serves as a museum and the headquarters for the park rangers. It is also the location of a number of paranormal manifestations. *Photo by Greg Latimer.*

The historic cemetery at Colonial Pemaquid, where some of the earliest European settlers to America lie in rest. *Photo by Greg Latimer.*

All that remains of a tragic tale lies here in the ruins of this foundation where a small home once stood at Colonial Pemaquid in the late 1600s. Archaeologists found a number of burned planks when they excavated this location, as well as a large number of bricks piled inside the north wall, indicating a chimney collapse there. The fire and destruction may have been accidental, or it may have occurred during the attacks of Native American Abenakis in 1676 or 1689. Either way, the structure was never rebuilt, according to archaeologists. *Photo by Greg Latimer.*

of a soldier in colonial uniform. As she watched in astonishment, the figure faded back into the unknown.

But perhaps the most compelling locations at the site are more haunting than haunted. A visitor to the cemetery can read markers that attest to the short life spans of the early settlers and the high death rate among children.

Just yards away, one can see the remnants of stone foundations for the houses of these settlers. They are miserably small, and it's easy to imagine whole families crowded into them as cold nor'easter winds blew in during the winter months.

Somewhere in the collective heart of all Americans, no matter where they emigrated from, one can feel both pride and sorrow in the hardships that generations have endured to build this country. Perhaps an even greater source of pride and sorrow are the depredations endured by the "First Americans"—the Native Americans—who continued to help build this country in spite of a history of broken treaties. One may want to consider this on a visit to the interior of Fort Henry to witness the rock on which a truce-seeking Native American spent his final hours in chains and wish him peace as perhaps he still makes his eternal walk to a shoreline tree, gazing out on the sea and freedom.

Chapter 13

Haunted Wiscasset Library Home to Multiple Spirits

With a coat of white paint over the bricks from which it is built, classically combined with Yankee-style black shutters and set off a bit from the street just enough to be framed by nearby trees, the Wiscasset Public Library doesn't have the immediate appearance of a location with multiple haunts. But even a former librarian concedes it just might be.

The structure was originally built in 1805 for the Lincoln and Kennebec Bank at the northeast end of High Street, a tree-lined road with a number of historic homes. Banking laws at the time, under the Massachusetts Charter of 1802, required that the bank maintain a reserve of "$100,000 in specie," a term that refers to assets in coin or bullion rather than notes.

Of course, the bank's proprietors needed to keep these assets safe from those who might seek to criminally appropriate them, so a vault, of sorts, was constructed.

In the northwest corner of the basement was a "Jug Vault," a brick structure said to have resembled a large bean pot, the top of which was entered through a trapdoor in the floor of the room above. This room is now the library Reading Room.

Additional research done by librarian Janet Morgan, a published author specializing in crime novels, revealed that the bankers had taken further steps to protect their precious specie. They had constructed a booby trap that would most likely cause the death of anyone attempting to break in to the vault.

The trap was created by digging a hollow space between the cellar walls and the jug vault in the corner of the building where the vault was placed.

The Wiscasset Library, where paranormal activity has been reported. *Photo by Greg Latimer.*

This hollow space was then filled with water, creating a moat between the outside wall and the jug vault.

Conceivably, anyone trying to dig into the vault from the outside walls in the corner would breach the moat and drown. However, while the historical record remains unclear if this ever occurred, local legend holds that there was a fatality, an accidental one, resulting in the death of a child.

According to the legend Morgan researched, a young boy was sent down to enter the vault near closing time for the bank. Exactly why a young boy was sent on this mission is never quite made clear. Apparently, the young lad was forgotten as the bank was closed up for the day, and he remained sealed in the vault overnight. When the vault was opened in the morning, the boy was found dead.

If the spirit of this unfortunate child haunts the book-lined aisles and antique-furnished rooms of the Wiscasset Public Library, he may find himself with otherworldly company, according to reports.

For some years, the second floor was leased to the county for offices of the Clerk of Courts, the Registry of Probate and the Registry of Deeds. Records were kept there until 1862 when Isaac T. Hobson converted the building to a private residence.

Under Hobson's ownership, a succession of several families resided in the former bank until 1929, when the building was purchased by a committee for use as the Wiscasset Public Library.

Perhaps the building continues to be visited by a member of these families, or as some reports assert, it may be the next-door neighbor. There are others who claim the spirit of a devoted library supporter may still haunt the location. All of these assertions revolve around multiple reports of an apparitional woman appearing in a window in the northeast corner of the second story at the library.

In a 2004 report in the Rockland *Courier-Gazette*, for which the reporter was accompanied by members of the Maine Paranormal Research Association (MPRA, now defunct), the apparition is said to be that of a woman who watches over her children.

According to MPRA co-director Nancy Caswell, the historical record indicates that a widower with thirteen children lived in the house next door to the library. There is no indication of how or when the mother of these children died, but it must have been an untimely and tragic demise to have left such a large family behind. Caswell said that two of the group's psychics assessed the area of the haunting and identified the entity there as the mother of the family, eternally peering from the second-story window, watching her many children at play in the yard below.

Another person who claimed to be sensitive to paranormal presences (not associated with MPRA) believes that another female presence haunts the second floor of the library and that this spirit is that of a woman who was a major library supporter who donated many items to the library that are still in the building.

The room located in the northern half of the second floor at the Wiscasset Public Library is the Hortense and Henry Ferne II Memorial Fine Arts Room, and perhaps it is the spirit of Hortense, continuing to watch over her collection. The room is considered by many to be the most outstanding private art library in northern New England.

Many topics are covered under the broad subject of arts. The Fine Arts Room holds information on architecture; landscape design; handicrafts such as crochet, knitting, weaving, quilting and needlepoint; technique guides; painting; sculpture; drawing; photography; and more. Books on all artistic mediums and artists are housed in this collection.

A room in the upstairs area of the Wiscasset Library where the apparition of a woman is sometimes seen looking out the windows. *Photo by Greg Latimer.*

There is comfortable seating, and an antique octagonal table provides a large surface for examining the books and prints. The display of original art on the walls adds to the enjoyment of the room, and the display case holds many of Hortense Ferne's tools and sketchbooks.

On a sunny day, the room is bathed in warm light from the windows, and visitors can usually relax in solitude and let their minds wander.

For those so inclined, they may also feel the presence of a devoted mother still watching over her children, a devout library supporter who contributed her beloved collection to the room or the lost spirit of a little boy spending the final moments of his life sealed in the terrifying darkness of the brick vault below.

Chapter 14
GHOST LIGHT OF THE MARSH RIVER

Two fishermen working a river tide in the gloom of a cold Maine night encountered a strange light that suddenly ascended into the night sky before disappearing into the darkness, leaving both of them frightened and mystified. A ghost? A UFO? Or perhaps a natural occurrence of some kind?

Fifteen years later, the incident remains unexplained, and one of the fishermen refuses to even talk about the episode. The fisherman who is willing to discuss the event tells a tale that compares with other incidents of "ghost lights" from around the world. A recent incident either adds to an explanation or contributes to the mystery.

The story begins as a fisherman we'll call Mike and his unidentified partner pull on their rubber waders, pick up their dip nets and prepare to slosh along muddy banks of the Marsh River in Newcastle in search of "elvers." Elvers are the second stage in the life cycle of the American eel (*Anguilla rostrata*), sometimes known as glass eels. The term is derived from the old English word "ellfare," which literally meant "eel journey."

Beginning their life as flat, transparent larvae shaped like willow leaves, the eels then grow into elvers as they approach the continental shelf. Beginning in the late winter months and continuing through the summer, the elvers migrate from the ocean into streams and estuaries, such as the Marsh River, a tidal estuary.

Fisheries for adult eels have a long history in Maine, having occurred since the earliest colonial settlements. The elver fishery is relatively recent, having begun in the early 1970s and operating up to 1978 and

The Marsh River in Newcastle, where late-night fishermen observed a "ghost light" rising above the marsh and a UFO was recently photographed. *Photo by Greg Latimer.*

recommencing in the early 1990s, according to the Maine Department of Marine Resources.

These, slender, delicate-looking creatures, about six to eight inches long, are highly valued in the Far East, where they are cultured and reared to adult size for the food market. An elver fisherman in Maine can earn hundreds of dollars for just a pound of live elvers, which is what brought Mike and his partner out into a chill winter night. Late-season snow flurries were dancing in the chill wind that blew around the fishermen as they activated their headlamps and started trudging toward their fishing spot.

It was a standard night out for the pair: cold and miserable. "They were long cold boring nights, often with snow flurries, frozen feet and hands, wet cigarettes and out in the middle of nowhere," Mike said.

Clearing the grassy areas along the riverside, the pair made their way through deep mud that sucked back on their rubber boots with each advancing step until they made it to their fishing spot. Once there, they went to work plunging their dip nets into the tidal flow of the Marsh River's dark waters in hopes of extracting some valuable elvers.

"All the land around us was either bog or grassland, and hillocks of pine," Mike said of their surroundings. "There were no houses or habitation other than occasional hunters or fishermen…We'd see a lot of wildlife, but not too many other folks."

Which is why they were a bit surprised when, after they had been working for several hours, they noticed what they first thought to be a camp-style lantern appear at location about one hundred yards away.

They knew that area to be where a railroad trestle crossed the river. "Once in a great while, we'd see someone take the long muddy trek to the railroad bridge," Mike said. "But since they never came back with much, we were never tempted to try our luck out there."

The pair wondered what hapless fisherman must be out on the trestle with the lantern, and they stopped briefly to watch the light, which was stationary and glowing white in the distance.

The two men returned to the task at hand, scooping with their nets and delivering any captured elvers to the bucket of water they kept nearby.

"After about a half hour, the lantern started to move down the tracks," Mike said. "We speculated they must not have done too well and were trying the other side where the channel was probably deeper."

Then they noticed that the light had begun to move to and fro, as though someone was walking along the railroad tracks swinging it with one arm. This observation brought about a new curiosity in the men. How could someone move so easily in the dark of night along the uneven terrain of the railroad tracks?

The light was making steady, even progress, which they thought would be impossible. Instead, they would expect to see such progress in a halting manner, with the walker having to slow or stop in order to examine the ground in front of him.

Both of them knew that missteps in this terrain could result in severe injuries, costing the victims' valuable time during the short elver season as well as creating unaffordable hospital bills.

This unusual observation caused both men to give their full attention to the light. It continued to move along the trestle area at a steady pace. According to Mike, "we started hooting rude encouragement," to whoever the walker might be, but they received no response.

Suddenly the light did something completely unexpected, and "that's when we shut up," Mike said.

The night seemed to grow even quieter as the men watched, astonished. "The light, still slightly swinging back and forth, started to rise, still at that same slow walking pace," Mike said, adding, "It's possible to climb to the top of the trestle but not keep that light swinging like if you were walking."

The men were further confounded by what happened next. "It was at this point that the light was starting to go way up above the top of the trestle and stopped swinging back and forth," Mike said. "Then I noticed splashing noises and turned around to see my buddy earnestly trying to be long gone."

As his fishing partner retreated through the mud and grass as quickly as possible, leaving his gear and the bucket of elvers behind, Mike stood his ground and watched the light in amazement. The strange light, no longer swinging at all, continued to rise in the night sky at slow, steady speed.

"It got too small to see when it got about a quarter of the way up from the horizon, going almost straight up in a slight arc, never changing its speed," Mike said.

He waited another half an hour, staring into the night sky and peering into the terrain around him to see if any other incidents might occur, but nothing happened.

"When I finally gave up waiting, I picked up mine and my buddy's equipment and went to my car," Mike said. "He was just sitting there, staring straight ahead, and refused to discuss anything. He was white as a sheet, thin-lipped and would look angry when I tried to discuss what we saw. In silence, I drove him home."

Mike's fishing partner never discussed the incident, and the man never returned to elver fishing. In fact, he never contacted Mike again. "To this day, I don't know if he saw something I didn't see or if the incident had some personal meaning for him," Mike said. "I guess I'll never know."

There was some speculation among Mike's friends that perhaps he had seen a ghostly railroad brakeman, carrying his lantern along the tracks before ascending into the heavens. If so, it may have been a one-time incident, as there have been no similar reports that might indicate the observation was a residual haunting.

A check of available records could not locate any incidents or accidents on that stretch of track that would support the possibility that a brakeman may have met his fate at the location.

However, there are several other possibilities for the strange light. The most obvious is that the glowing circle was a "ghost light" or "spook light." These are reported worldwide with a variety of names including "will of the wisp," "foxfire" and "elf light."

They are often associated with open marshy areas where they are attributed to "swamp gas," but the conditions at Marsh River in those chill nighttime hours after a long, cold winter were not conducive to producing such gasses.

The strange lights go back into history, and they are often associated with sacred places. There is some speculation that these phenomena may have inspired the ancients regarding locations to build religious sites.

A temple was built in the western mountains of China to better observe the "Bodhisattva Lights." In 1937, writer John Blofeld described the lights at this location as "fluffy balls of orange-colored fire, moving through space, unhurried and majestic."

Orange balls were also seen in 1989 near the great stone circle of Avebury in England, which was constructed in 2600 BC. In 1919, similar lights were also observed in England at the Castlerigg Stone Circle, constructed in 3300 BC. An observer at Castlerigg said at the time, "We then saw a number of lights in the direction of the Druidical circle. Whilst we were watching, one of the lights came straight to the spot where we were standing; at first very faint, as it approached the light increased in intensity. When it came close it slowed down, stopped, quivered and slowly went out."

In early Wales, the lights were called "corpse candles" that were said to appear just above ground level at the exact height of a human hand rising from the soil. There was also the Welsh legend of "fairy fire" in which a small goblin-like fairy called a *púca* leads lone nighttime travelers at night off the beaten path so they become hopelessly lost.

Germans believed the floating lights were the ghosts of land thieves. In Finland, the lights were believed to be the ghosts of children who had been buried in the forest and were called *liekkio,* meaning "flaming one."

In Scandinavia, it was believed that these lights marked sites that were supposed to contain treasure, and in central Europe, they were regarded as the lost souls of stillborn children.

Ghost lights have been reported in the United States since the late 1800s. The first article in print featuring such lights was carried in the *Charlotte Observer* in 1913.

Of course, scientists have an explanation for these strange lights, but while their description is scientifically accurate, it doesn't explain all the incidents reported.

The phenomenon of "swamp gas" occurs when oxidized phosphine gas and methane mix as a byproduct of organic decay. When blended, these two compounds ignite and give off photon emissions. The result is the creation of phosphine, which then ignites as it comes into contact with oxygen. This smaller ignition then encounters the more abundant methane already in the air, creating a momentary ball of flame.

This type of ignition requires some heat in the environment, which was notably lacking at the Marsh River incident.

There is yet another phenomenon associated with such floating lights—unidentified flying objects (UFOs)—and the Marsh River has had a recent encounter with a possible UFO sighting.

In September 2013, Paula Roberts, sports editor of *The Lincoln County News*, was traveling between games when she spotted a bright object in the early evening sky near where the Marsh River crosses U.S. Route 1 in Newcastle.

Roberts, a lifetime resident of Lincoln County, felt that the object was out of place. She had made the same run between sporting events hundreds of times and had never seen anything like it. She got out of her car, grabbed her camera, which was already fitted with a 200-millimeter lens, and took several photos. When she examined the photo later, enlarging it on her computer screen, she found something she didn't expect and couldn't identify. "It was out of this world, like nothing I had ever seen," Roberts said at the time.

She described it as a "bright white object with no flashing lights, traveling in a straight line" to her right (the northern side of Route 1). She was also able to discern that there was no sound coming from the object's direction. Her photo reveals a small circular object that appears to have flat ridges around it.

The newspaper assigned a reporter to investigate the incident. He contacted the National Aeronautics and Space Administration (NASA) to ascertain if any satellites or the International Space Station were in the area at the time.

Steve Cole, with the NASA Office of Communications in Washington, D.C., advised that the possibility of a satellite being overhead at the time could not be completely eliminated. According to Cole, "We do not keep a comprehensive record of past satellite locations." He added that "even if we were to rule out any NASA satellites over that location at that time, there are a lot of other satellites up there."

However, Cole added a caveat. "One thing that can be safely said about any satellite as seen in the nighttime sky from Earth, it would appear as a fairly small point of light moving slowly but noticeably in an arc," Cole said. Roberts described the object as moving in a straight line at a good pace fairly low to the ground, not in a slow, high arc.

The next contact was with the Mutual UFO Network, known as MUFON. This is a group of nationally recognized and well-qualified volunteers dedicated to "the scientific study of UFOs for the benefit of humanity."

Three of the group's experts reviewed the photo and the circumstances surrounding it.

One MUFON expert found the photo inconclusive, and two MUFON experts ruled the image a commercial aircraft on approach to a nearby airport.

With two out of three MUFON investigators agreeing that the object was in fact an aircraft approaching an airport to the south, which would explain why it was lower to the ground than a high-flying aircraft in transit or a satellite, it would seem that the investigation was concluded. However, Greg Hughes of the nearby Portland (Maine) Jetport knocked that conclusion out of consideration.

"There shouldn't be anything coming from that direction," he said, pointing out that most of the arriving flights at the Jetport come from the south. "It just doesn't make sense that somebody would swing up that far," he said.

Hughes checked for arriving flights during that time of day and noted that the only flight was from Philadelphia, which is well south of Portland, Maine.

A check of FlightTracker.com for air traffic near the Jetport or over Newcastle during the time period between 6:00 p.m. and 8:00 p.m. on a Friday night also indicated that no commercial aircraft should have been in the area.

So what did Mike and his fishing partner observe over the Marsh River on that chill night? A visiting ghost? A natural phenomenon? A UFO? It will certainly never be known for sure. But Mike said he will always remember it as one of the strangest things he has ever seen. As for his fishing partner, who ran from the sighting in fright and would never speak of it, he is probably still trying to forget the Ghost Light of Marsh River.

Chapter 15

LADY OF THE NIGHT

Built in the 1840s, the building presently housing King Eiders Pub used to be a harness shop, a tavern and a soda fountain called "Clark's Spa." It was later the first location for Mexicali Blues, now a successful retail chain.

Past and some current employees have reported "creepy" feelings on the second floor. Passersby in the late-night hours claim to have a seen a light floating by the upstairs windows after the restaurant has closed. Others report that lights in the entire building are turned on after the place is closed, such as the time a delivery man called the owners in the early morning hours to ask why the whole restaurant was lit up. One of the owners was amazed. He had personally shut the restaurant down that night and had a vivid recollection of turning all the lights off.

According to locals, the upstairs used to be the apartment of a sailor and his wife. As a sailor often is, this one would often be gone for long periods time. Whether the sailor's wife needed a little extra money or just wanted company, she is said to have started a small business that some refer to as the "oldest profession." She may have signaled with a light from the top floor.

One night, the lady was murdered, and the crime has never been solved. Her husband may have come home unexpectedly. Or perhaps the murder was committed by a disgruntled customer.

The woman's body was found in the back part of the second floor, which is where many of the employees say they feel her presence. A short paranormal exploration of this area encountered electromagnetic field spikes in this area. Such EMF activity is thought to be associated with a paranormal presence.

The present-day King Eider's Pub in Damariscotta, where employees describe a haunting on the second floor thought to be that of a "lady of the night" who formerly occupied the building. The giant painted pumpkin on the patio is part of the Damariscotta Pumpkinfest and Regatta, an event that takes place every October in Newcastle and Damariscotta that involves decorating giant pumpkins for display on the street or hollowing them out to make boats and racing them on the Damariscotta River. The pumpkin in the photo was painted by Glenn Chadbourne, a Newcastle resident who is Stephen King's illustrator. *Photo by Greg Latimer.*

The upstairs room at King Eider's Pub in Damariscotta, where employees have described strange encounters with an entity thought to be that of a "lady of the night" who formerly plied her trade there. *Photo by Greg Latimer.*

Because many of the facts associated with this haunting have been lost to time, and confirmation of paranormal activity at this location may never be resolved, the possibility that King Eider's employees are welcoming guests during business hours while the ghostly Lady of the Night still puts a welcoming light out afterhours can never be completely disregarded. Either way, it's always worth a glance up at the second-story window when passing by King Eider's Pub on a cold Maine night.

Chapter 16
HISTORIC HOME, HAUNTED HANDYMAN?

A ny visitor passing through Damariscotta will almost certainly notice Schooner Landing on one side of Main Street at the Newcastle/ Damariscotta Bridge and a white Federal-style house with four columns supporting the portico on the other side of the street. These two locations are vestiges of one of the great pioneers of the Damariscotta area, Matthew Cottrill.

Although the present-day Schooner Landing serves the town as a restaurant and marina, it actually has been a landing for schooners since it was Cottrill's Wharf in the late 1700s. The modern facility is built on the same footprint as the old wharf, and some of the old materials that supported the structure are still present. When work was done recently at the site, an old unfinished headstone from the 1800s was found among the granite rocks and other detritus used as fill for the cribworks foundation. It was likely thrown away by the Page Memorial Company, formerly located across the street. The Cottrill House has been beautifully preserved by Dr. Joseph Griffin, DMD, whose office is at the location. He recently had the building repaired and repainted, all the while maintaining its historic look.

There have been a variety of reports regarding strange sightings and activity at the Cottrill House, some modern and some historic. In order to understand them better, it may be a good idea to examine some of the history behind this haunt.

As young men, Matthew Cottrill and his partner James Kavanaugh left County Wexford, Ireland, and went to sea. Some years later, they showed

The Matthew Cottrill House on Main Street, Damariscotta, where a number of strange occurrences have been reported. *Photo by Greg Latimer.*

up in Boston with a notable amount of money, for which the source is lost to time. The funds allowed them to establish themselves in the small Irish Catholic community in Boston and marry well. However, opportunities for young Irishmen in what was a Protestant-dominated Boston at the time were few and far between.

The two decided to board a northbound ship with their new wives and try their luck in northern New England. They landed near Bristol and headed up the Damariscotta River, where they saw the beginnings of a new community and plenty of opportunity in the twin villages of Damariscotta and Newcastle.

Kavanaugh and Cottrill opened a general mercantile store in 1788, likely in the same location as the Cottrill House, according to an old map in the Skidompha Library files.

The pair of Irish adventurers quickly went to work. By 1797, a French visitor to the area noted that the three-hundred-ton ship *Hibernia* was under construction at the Kavanaugh-Cottrill yard. In 1799, the men were members of a group that built the first Damariscotta/Newcastle Bridge.

By 1800, they had built twenty-five ships that were plying the West Indies lumber trade, where some cargoes brought as much as $40,000. They used profits to pay off the mortgage on a large plot of land they had acquired, and then they turned their attention to their dwellings.

Local legend has it that they somehow shanghaied a talented architect named Nicholas Codd from Ireland and brought him straight over to Damariscotta aboard one of the ships in their fleet.

Codd built Cottrill's home first, a two-story house perched on a granite foundation at the present Main Street location. The arched window above the portico offered Cottrill a full view of the activities at his shipyard.

Codd later built a mansion for Kavanaugh, as well as St. Patrick's Church, both in the Damariscotta Mills area, and both are still standing in fine condition.

Likewise, the Cottrill House is still in fine shape even after hundreds of stormy winters and simmering summers. Several unusual tales are associated with it. The earliest is a tale of lost treasure.

The Matthew Cottrill House on Main Street, Damariscotta, in an undated photo likely taken in the 1950s due to the presence of both parking meters and elm trees. (The elm trees were later all killed by Dutch elm disease.) The building is considered one of the finest examples of Federal architecture in the United States. It was designed by Nicholas Codd, who was brought in from Ireland by Cottrill and his business partner, James Kavanaugh. Codd also designed St. Patrick's Catholic Church under the direction of Kavanaugh and Cottrill, presently the oldest surviving Catholic church in New England. *Photo courtesy of the Damariscotta Historical Society.*

According to a newspaper article written in 1901, a group of workmen under the supervision of George Jones were renovating the Cottrill House and located an iron kettle under the floor. Before they could open it, Jones grabbed it and took it away. Rumors circulated around town that the kettle contained over $11,000 in gold, but Jones wouldn't reveal what, if anything, he found inside.

Some fifty years later, a man who identified himself as part of the Jones crew told a Damariscotta resident that indeed the kettle was full of old coins and that Jones had immediately seized it. In his haste, Jones neglected to see one of the coins drop to the floor, and the workman had been able to retrieve it.

Another story, this time with a paranormal twist, is said to have occurred in the mid-1900s when the home was occupied by the Dr. Rufus Stetson, his family and, perhaps, the ghost of their handyman.

Mrs. Stetson was very fastidious when it came to cleanliness in her house, and she absolutely hated rats. Unfortunately, these nasty rodents made occasional appearances around the house.

The Stetsons employed a handyman who took care of chopping wood, yard work and other chores, but he knew that one of his primary jobs was to keep the property rat free.

One day, he found a nest and told Mrs. Stetson about it. He said that he had a plan to be rid of it and would begin the next day. Unfortunately, the handyman passed away that very evening.

Mrs. Stetson immediately hired another handyman and made it clear to him that his most important job would be to keep the place rat-free and that he was to start the next day.

That night, Mrs. Stetson had a dream that she was standing at the head of her beautiful flying staircase, looking down at rats running around all over her polished floors in the foyer. She grabbed a broom and began hitting them, sweeping them out the front door.

In the morning, she didn't seem to remember this dream at all and was going about her normal morning routine when the new handyman knocked at the door. She was glad to see him and reminded him of his most important job: the rats.

Looking a bit surprised, he turned and looked back toward the front door with a grin and said, "That should be easy—there are three dead ones right here!"

Mrs. Stetson's dream came back to her all at once, and she was horrified that she might have really been in the midst of all those rats in the hall during the overnight hours. She ran back to her husband's medical office to tell him about the incident but was too upset to speak. Dr. Stetson sedated her and laid her on his fainting couch. After a spell, she was able to calm down and told her husband about her dream.

He went with her to look and sure enough there were three dead rats on the front porch. Did she really kill them? Even Mrs. Stetson never seemed to know for sure.

However, local legend asserts that no other rats have been seen on the property since the handyman's death and Mrs. Stetson's dream. Some say it's the conscientious handyman who died before he could finish his job, hanging around keeping the rats away even after his own death.

If so, it may also explain why the Cottrill House always looks so well kept. Perhaps the good Dr. Griffin has some help from a haunted handyman.

Chapter 17

THE WATCHER OF DODGE POINT

Before human existence in the Twin Villages, when time was without definition, there was only the land and the sea, and much of the land was covered with glacial ice. Then, some eleven thousand years ago, the glaciers began to recede, with one of them gouging a streambed into the rocky coastal ledge to create the Damariscotta River.

The glacial retreat left behind a new river surrounded by a meager terrain of tundra and sparse spruce woodlands, but it was enough to support game and forage. It was then that the first people came, with the earliest known as the "Red Paint People," named after the red ferrous oxide used in their burials.

They were followed by others. In the Damariscotta area, they were known as Abenakis, although they more probably referred to themselves as "Etchamin" or "the people," a Native American tradition in the area.

The emotional and historical connection of these people with the land and river was strong and may live on today in the form of an apparitional Native American who continues to watch over Dodge Point in Newcastle.

A local resident we'll call Graham regularly walks the trails in the area, and he reports that, on several occasions, he has seen the Watcher of Dodge Point.

"He gives off a feeling of peace but also of immense, powerful strength, both personally and in perceived energy," Graham said. "I always have a strong sense that he is watching out for the health of the woods and keeping the peace here."

A view of Dodge Point from the Damariscotta River. *Photo by Olga Oros/damariscottarivercruises.com.*

Graham describes the apparition as a well-proportioned male dressed in leather buckskins without beads, feathers or other décor. He is not seen carrying weapons but is somehow able to communicate that he is peaceful but strong, Graham said.

Two sightings have been reported by Graham, both in daylight hours. One was halfway up the well-marked Ravine Trail in the area, and the other occurred while Graham was "busting brush" off the trail close to Dodge Cove.

In both cases, Graham said that the sighting began in his peripheral vision—not an uncommon occurrence when dealing with the paranormal.

According to an article by Patricia Hogarty on chronicle.com (the website for the out-of-print *San Francisco Chronicle*), peripheral vision may have advantages in perceiving a paranormal presence.

"The images you sense on the edge of your sight, from the corner of your eye, is your peripheral vision. Paranormal investigators often work on using their peripheral vision, because it is a popular belief that it's the best way to see the shadowy forms of spirits," Hogarty noted.

"Our eyes see with two types of preceptor cells: cone cells and rod cells. Rod cells are unable to distinguish color and are predominant at the periphery, while cone cells are concentrated mostly in the center of the retina. Peripheral vision is especially useful at night or in the dark, when the lack of color cues and lighting makes cone cells far less useful. And, peripheral vision is particularly good at sensing motion," Hogarty wrote.

According to studies done by Tennessee-based Paranormal Technology Investigations (PTI), "Seeing an object/shadow out of the corner of your eye, then when you turn you head to make eye contact and discover nothing is there is very common, and it is also a very commonly missed piece of paranormal activity that we neglect to realize."

The staff members at PTI assert that images seen with peripheral vision are accurate, but that they may not be as visible when viewed straight on. They suggest, "Next time you think you see the shadow, or small or large object or whatever it might be you think you're seeing through your peripherals, pay attention to it. Try to continue watching it through your peripherals, because chances are when you do decide to turn & look at it head on, you're not going to see it."

Dodge Point would be a likely place for a watchful guardian to haunt. The point is home to Native American shell heaps and is just downriver from the largest shell heaps in the world, at the Glidden Midden in Newcastle and the Whaleback Midden in Damariscotta. These middens are on opposite sides of the Damariscotta River and are essentially part of the same site. The size and range of Native American activity in this area extends far beyond the well-defined piles easily recognized by visitors. Hikers on trails hundreds of yards away will often find themselves walking over ancient shells compressed into the earth.

Shell middens are essentially enormous garbage heaps, and many items of interest have been dug out of the middens on the Damariscotta River. Pottery shards, primitive tools, fish bones and even human remains have been excavated from the middens.

The middens were formed by a chemical process that contributed to their longevity. The molecular makeup of the shells that contributed to most of the midden content made the surrounding soil much less acidic, which chemically prevented the soil from breaking down, causing these middens to remain intact for centuries. Even today, oyster shells are a prized local favorite for crushing into dirt driveways, causing the ground to harden.

The geography of Dodge Point would also make it attractive to Native American hunters and gatherers. Not only are the woods full of game (even today), but the 508-acre peninsula is also home to a variety of medicinal and food plants that would have been valuable to Native Americans.

Native American fishermen would also have been attracted to Dodge Point because of the variety of shoreline environments. On the northern edge of the property is a shallow inlet now called Brickyard Cove. As one walks farther south along the shoreline, there is a small beach area with a mud shoal that extends into the river and is exposed at low tide. Further along the eastern shore, there is a precipitous drop off from the riverbank that allows a shore fisherman access to deep water. Dodge Point is a popular destination for striped bass fishermen today, and it is most likely that these prized food fish were far more plentiful during the time period when Native Americans populated the area.

The Dodge Point area is also a great place for a leisurely hike and is filled with history from the early European population.

The well-forested reserve, maintained by the Damariscotta River Association (DRA), is accessible from River Road in Newcastle. The land slopes gently down from a 240-foot height of land to the Damariscotta River, offering views downriver that extend for miles. The property is rich in ecological and historical values as well as scenic beauty. There are old-growth trees and several important plant communities.

The Dodge Point trail is an easy hike along old trails used by residents since the 1800s. It winds through a mixed-growth forest with gentle slopes and a large stand of red pine. Along the way, it passes old stone walls, remnants of farmers' property boundaries. There is also an ice pond off this trail that was used by past residents of the area during the winter to obtain ice for their iceboxes for cold storage prior to the introduction of electricity.

Dodge Point was the site of a historic brick-making operation in the late 1800s. In May 1890, the *Damariscotta Herald* reported that eleven million bricks were manufactured for the annual season, employing two hundred men and a market for five thousand cords of wood and 180 vessels for transportation. Dodge Point was one of the largest of these brickyards.

The unusually good Pleistocene clay along the river was laid down by glaciers and left iron oxide in the muddy riverbank, which is what gave the bricks their red color.

The area of Brickyard Cove is still strewn with brick "wasters," and the adjacent woods conceal clay fire pits. The bricks were formed by packing brick clay into wooden forms and then drying them under the sun. The bricks were then built into a huge beehive pile, layering the bricks with wood. Then the "hive" was set on fire. Many of the "wasters" still lining the shore at Dodge Point were made when this less-than-efficient method caused them to crack, over-cook or collapse.

The bricks that survived this process were considered to be of good quality. These were layered in high trays that could be slid onto the ships that pulled up to the Dodge Point beach at low tide. Bricks from the Damariscotta River helped build Boston; New York; Portland, Maine; and Halifax, Canada.

Those who would like to personally visit both Dodge Point and the Whaleback Midden will find easily accessible parking areas and well-marked trails maintained by the DRA, a nonprofit group that protects and manages more than 2,900 acres of land and twenty-two miles of fresh- and saltwater shoreline in the area.

The trailhead for the Dodge Point trails is three miles south of downtown Damariscotta on River Road in Newcastle. A map of all four trails is available at a kiosk in the parking area.

The trailhead for the Whaleback Midden is located on Upper Main Street (Business Route 1) in Damariscotta near Biscay Road. An informative kiosk with a trail map is located in the parking area.

While there is much to see while wandering through these areas, it is also an interesting experience to clear one's mind of the modern surroundings and imagine the area when it was home to early Native Americans. While one is surveying the land, and perhaps watching the graceful flight of an eagle or osprey, it may also be prudent to check one's peripheral vision to see if he or she, too, may be under surveillance by the ghostly Watcher of Dodge Point.

Chapter 18

HAUNTED HALLWAYS OF THE
LINCOLN COUNTY COURTHOUSE

Central to the riverside village of Wiscasset is the Lincoln County Courthouse, constructed in 1824. The courthouse building was fashioned in the Georgian style of architecture, and it is patterned after old English buildings. Additions in 1950 and 1972 were performed with careful regard to match and complement the original structure, and most residents feel the result was a success.

Walking up the granite stairs and entering the Superior Court hearing room is like taking steps back in time. The beautifully appointed room looks much as it did when it first opened to the public. Still remaining in the courtroom are the circular niches in which the stoves stood and a marvelous old curved bench. In the jury room, there are antique chairs and a table. When the judge enters the bench area from his chambers and strikes his gavel, he is calling to order the oldest courthouse in Maine in which court is still held.

There is more history in the ground-level hallway, where a variety of historical artifacts are on display, including scales used in 1856 to test weights and measures.

Old, well-maintained buildings filled with period items are natural attractions for ghostly entities seeking to continue their existence in familiar surroundings, according to paranormal researchers. So it was no surprise when reports and a compelling video surfaced about paranormal activity at the old courthouse.

One longtime courthouse employee had experienced continual manifestations during her tenure there. Often required to work after regular

The Lincoln County Courthouse in Wiscasset, where employees have described paranormal incidents and a round object was taped by security cameras floating about the hallways and right through solid wood doors and walls. *Photo by Greg Latimer.*

business hours, when the building was quiet and empty, she could hear footsteps in a stairwell and elevators moving between floors. Upon investigation, she would find no one in the areas.

The elevator hauntings, in particular, have been attributed to the spirit of woman who loved the building and was a dedicated volunteer and benefactor of restoration efforts.

In May 1975, while going about her volunteer duties, the woman suddenly collapsed and died in an elevator. While emergency medical technicians were rushing her to a hospital in an attempt to save her, they forgot one of her shoes in the elevator, and it was subsequently lost in the confusion. Courthouse lore is that the lady returns to the elevator seeking her lost shoe, but it may be more logical that the dedication of this volunteer simply continues, albeit in a more ethereal form.

There is another shadowy form that may be haunting the courthouse, and it is known to disregard orders from the police.

The story behind this recent incident begins with police being dispatched to the building in regard to a possible intruder while the court was closed. In standard police procedure, one officer went to the front door, and a second officer went to the back door. The officer responding to the back door found a suspect there and took him into custody. At almost the same moment, the officer responding to the front door reported he could see the figure of a man inside the entrance and disappearing within the building's interior. A perimeter was established to prevent the additional suspect from leaving the building, and a thorough search was performed. No one was found.

The elusive figure remained a mystery. Had a second suspect somehow escaped? Or had the officer encountered one of the courthouse spirits?

In another incident at the courthouse, there was no problem observing the object in question. It was recorded by a courthouse security camera.

Courthouse technicians were checking videotapes in an effort to ascertain why some of the recently installed cameras in the building weren't functioning properly. Almost accidentally, they noticed something strange.

At 6:18 p.m. on September 27, 2011, a camera that had been off suddenly switched on, apparently activated by its motion detector system. From the lower right corner of the screen, a misty circular object appeared, emanating from a solid wall. It wandered down the hallway, made a turn, passed through a closed wooden door into a room and then returned to view by passing through the same door back into the hallway.

It glided farther back up the hallway toward the camera and then stopped momentarily. Then it turned and passed through another solid wooden door. This time it did not reappear, and after some seconds without movement in the hallway, the camera automatically shut down. The whole scene lasted about seven seconds.

Very little can be discerned about the object from simply viewing the tape, but two aspects about the object are obvious. The object's presence was substantial enough to activate the motion detector on the camera, which is more than a bug or small mouse could do, according to the technicians at the courthouse. The object also appears to be seen in proper perspective as it moved up and down the hallway. The perspective is visually enhanced by a long mat bordered by checkerboard floor tiles.

Security cameras monitoring this hallway at the Lincoln County Courthouse on September 27, 2011, captured a circular object moving down the hall and passing through solid walls and doors. *Photo by Greg Latimer.*

"When we first saw the tape, we didn't know what to make of it, but as we continued to review it, it became apparent that there was definitely something there," said county commissioner chair Sheridan Bond, who reviewed the tape with the entire board, in 2011. "We sure didn't know what it was, and we still don't."

Upon review (the video can generally be found online by entering "courthouse ghost Wiscasset Maine" in a search engine), the most striking behavior of the circular object was not just its ability to pass through solid objects but why it was doing so.

The area where the object was spotted is part of the courthouse additions, which means the object may have been following a residual path established before the addition was built, causing it to pass through walls that were nonexistent at the time it was with the living.

A residual haunting occurs when a spirit continues to dwell at a location, stuck in time and repeating its actions over and over. There is speculation that the spirits are unaware that they are deceased. They do not interact with anyone or anything, just continue on their lonely, eternal mission.

The evanescent object seen on the video may also be referred to as an "orb," a circular object sometimes seen in photos and videos but not with the naked eye. A more detailed discussion about orbs is available in chapter 12 of this book, "Haunts and History of the Ancient Burial Ground."

Very much like the residual haunting described above, life and work goes on at the historic Lincoln County Courthouse every weekday. Papers are filed, courtroom dramas played out and fates decided. And, perhaps, somewhere within those walls, a dedicated volunteer goes about her ghostly business, a shadowy figure moves in stealth and an unseen object follows its route through the walls, all in the haunted hallways of the Lincoln County Courthouse.

Chapter 19

HAUNTS OF THE FORMER MAINE HOTEL

W hat was once the grandest hotel in the town of Damariscotta continues to be a thriving retail and residential location, and it is also home to a few resident spirits, according to reports.

Originally constructed in 1850 by shipbuilder Joseph Day Jr. as a Greek Revival structure, the Day Block on Main Street still stands as a fine example of success, not only because of the current business and residential presence but also as a wonderful historic representation.

During the building's early days, it was home to the Maine Hotel, Damariscotta's finest spot for dining or lodging. According to records of the Alna Lodge of the Freemasons in Damariscotta, there was a "well attended" public installation of officers at the hotel's banquet room on the second floor of the building "to which the ladies were invited," on November 29, 1854.

"An excellent supper was served and all present seemed to enjoy the evening's entertainment and expressed very great satisfaction," according to description.

The building changed hands several times, and by 1925, the hotel operations ended. However, it was still an important building, with the First National Bank, the post office and a barbershop located on the ground floor. The upstairs rooms were rented as offices and apartments.

Due in large part to the efforts of the Freeman family, who purchased and began restoring the property in 1962, the Day Block still provides an attractive and profitable structure right in the middle of downtown.

Storefronts and the entrance (between columns in the center of the photo) for the Maine Hotel on Main Street, Damariscotta. The building is now the Day Block Apartments, where several eerie incidents have been reported. *Photo courtesy of the Damariscotta Historical Society.*

The Day Block on Main Street in Damariscotta, formerly the Maine Hotel. The location has a long history and several tales of mystery. *Photo by Greg Latimer.*

In 1980, the building was acquired by Ralph and Judy Doering of the Day Block Trust, who continue to maintain the structure in good condition and make additional improvements.

Any building with a long history of public occupation is certainly susceptible to residency from "the other side" as well, and the Day Block has at least two interesting reports from past residents.

One resident had lived in the building for quite a number of years. He remembered that on occasion he would catch the scent of what he described as "cheap, awful perfume" wafting through the stairwell as he walked up to his apartment. He took very little notice of it, assuming that there was a resident somewhere in the building who favored the malodorous scent as part of her personal grooming.

As time went on, he continued to catch the scent in the air, and he continued to disregard it, except to pick up his pace as he climbed the stairs—as long as it didn't require him to inhale any more deeply.

This continued for a number of years, until one afternoon, breathing a little more heavily as he lugged some groceries up the stairs, he caught the distinctive scent yet again. A thought struck that caused him to pause in the stairwell in spite of vile odor. He realized that he had lived in the building long enough that all of the women renting apartments when he originally moved in had left the building. So why was the perfume still around?

He asked some acquaintances to check the stairwell, and sure enough, some of them caught the distinctive scent as well.

While not as dramatic as a full-bodied apparition, olfactory manifestation has been recognized by paranormal experts for some time. "Phantosmia," as paranormal investigators refer to the phenomenon, is relatively common and can be associated with good or comforting scents, as well as foul perfumes and cigar or cigarette odors.

A hallway at the Day Block apartments in Damariscotta, where the odor of a mysterious (and not too pleasing) perfume continues to surprise residents and visitors. The strange odor has continued, on and off, for over ten years (at least), despite the fact that no single resident has been in the building for that long. *Photo by Greg Latimer.*

Dave (no last name given), the lead investigator and case manager for Connecticut-based Manchester Paranormal Investigations, recalled one experience.

"Our favorite olfactory apparitions happened to us during one of our investigations last year. When we sensed a spirit was around we then smelled an old-fashioned cologne smell. The spirit was invited to follow us around and that we knew it was him because of the smell. He followed us the entire evening," Dave wrote in a 2011 posting on the group's website.

Libby Tucker, folklore teacher and the author of *Haunted Halls*, an interpretive study of college ghost lore, described an encounter in New Orleans:

A friend of my sister Sarah once rented an apartment in the French quarter of New Orleans that had odd smells. Some hot summer days when she got home from work, Sarah's friend found that her apartment smelled like stale beer and cheap lilac perfume. Each time she encountered these smells, Sarah's friend would open all the windows and air the apartment out. Finally she asked her landlord if he could help solve her odor problem. "I don't think so," her landlord said. "Many years ago a sailor visited the woman he loved here in this apartment. His girlfriend always wore lilac perfume. One day, after he'd been drinking beer, the sailor found his girlfriend with another man. He killed both of them on the spot, then killed himself. The smell of stale beer is the sailor's ghost, and the smell of cheap lilac perfume is his girlfriend's. There's no way you can get rid of those smells." Soon after hearing this story, Sarah's friend moved to a new place with no spectral roommates.

The second incident described at the Day Block was much less odiferous and a bit more frightening. It involved an apparently ghostly visitor who enjoyed a good rocking chair.

A young woman was alone, except for the company of her deaf dog, in her Day Block apartment one evening, waiting for her mother's return. The woman was sitting on the couch, reading. She noticed that the dog got up and focused on a rocking chair in the room, which she thought was strange because of the dog's being deaf.

The next thing she knew, the rocking chair started rocking. The woman was sure the chair hadn't been bumped by the dog. Not sure exactly what was happening and not knowing how to respond, the woman just put her feet up on the couch and watched.

Soon the rocker slowed down, and just then, she heard the front door open and slam. Relieved that her mother was apparently home, she ran to greet her and tell her what had happened, but the entryway was empty. She opened the door and looked out into the hallway, finding no one there either.

Lost in disbelief, she returned to the apartment interior, where the chair had stopped rocking, and the dog had calmed down. Shaking her head, she settled back into reading her book, knowing that later she would have one heck of story for her mother about a haunting at the former Maine Hotel.

Chapter 20
THE VOYEUR PORTRAIT

The Disney cartoon character Bambi, a lovable fawn who survives woodland tragedy and disaster on his path to triumph, is well known to generations of children. What is less known is the special role played by a Damariscotta resident in the creation of this iconic character and the paranormal event experienced by his wife in their home.

Family members still associated with the home and visitors to the building have described a playful spirit haunting the location, and "playful" was certainly the mood when the "Voyeur Portrait" came to life in the house. The historic home, located at 20 Bristol Road in Damariscotta, was built for the Daniel Day family in 1798. Daniel owned a busy shipyard nearby and was active in community affairs, as well as a church deacon. Even after his death in 1849, portraits of him and his wife continued to hang on the second-floor hallway of the Day House, both wearing the dour facial expressions that were common for portraits of the period.

Successive generations of the Day family have continued to occupy the Day house, and one of these was Maurice "Jake" Day, sometimes called Damariscotta's Bambi connection. Jake showed early promise in the arts while he attended high school at Lincoln Academy in Newcastle. After graduation, he attended the Massachusetts College of Art, where he studied painting and drawing. Later, he transferred to the school of the Museum of Fine Arts in Boston and graduated in 1915.

Jake saw military service with the army on the Mexican border and then with the navy in its camouflage department (where his artistic skills were likely put to good use).

The Day House in Damariscotta, where there is a history of paranormal occurrences, including one in which a painting of the Day family patriarch seemed to be smiling at a scantily clad woman leaving the shower. *Photo by Greg Latimer.*

Jake Day's wood carving studio, which was set apart from the main house, shown during a snowy Maine winter. Although the photo is undated, it was most likely taken in the 1950s when Day returned to Damariscotta after helping create the Bambi character for Walt Disney and helping to illustrate many Disney animated films. While the shack has been bulldozed, the original Day House built in 1798 is still standing and includes a gallery of Day's work. Some visitors to the gallery have reported paranormal occurrences, including a disembodied voice saying, "Slow down and look," one of Day's favorite phrases. *Photo courtesy of the Damariscotta Historical Society.*

After the war ended, Jake returned to Damariscotta and began illustrating for a variety of publications. According to his obituary in the *New York Times*, Jake provided illustrations for the *Atlantic Monthly*, *Vanity Fair* and *Life* magazines in this early stage of his career. He also illustrated books for Henry Beston, Elizabeth Coatsworth and Edmund Ware Smith.

A prolific artist, sculptor, photographer and naturalist, his work mirrored his passion for Maine's landscapes and creatures. Also known as "Colonel Jake" of "Jake's Rangers," he and his band of local sportsmen were central characters in many of Edmund Ware Smith's hunting and fishing stories.

In 1928, Jake and his wife, Beatrice, had recently celebrated their tenth anniversary with a "tin wedding." Since the couple was well known and well liked in the town, a large number of friends surprised them with a party, including a ride on a wooden chariot in which the pair was hauled about town.

Some days after this event, a quiet summer afternoon found the couple going about their separate tasks in the Day House. Jake was immersed in his artwork on the ground floor of the building. Beatrice, in preparation for a social engagement that evening, was enjoying a relaxing bath in a chamber on the second floor.

When Beatrice finished her bath, she dried off and entered the hallway that led to her dressing room. No one was quite sure what she was wearing, but according to a description from Damariscotta historian Harold Castner, it would appear that she was clad in little or nothing. After all, except for her husband downstairs, there was no one else in the house, and it was just a short walk to the dressing room down the hall, passing in front of the portraits of family patriarch Daniel Day and his wife.

As she made the short walk down the hall to her dressing room door, she became aware of what felt like a tapping on her right shoulder that grew stronger and steadier as she approached the door.

Stopping abruptly at the entryway in irritation, she turned around to see what sort of flying insect or drafty breeze could be causing the annoying feeling on her shoulder. Looking about quickly, she saw nothing—until she noticed the portrait of Daniel Day.

According to Castner's description, she momentarily froze in place, gasping. The portrait of the old deacon was doing something completely uncharacteristic: he was smiling at her, an admiring smile.

She instinctively moved her hands to cover her breasts and then turned and ran into the room, collapsing on the bed. After regaining her composure and pulling on some clothes, she inched back toward the door and opened it. The portrait had returned to the usual dour look. She called her husband up from his labors on the first floor and told him what had happened. He looked at her and the portrait in disbelief. A typical Jake response would have been to shake his head and smile. But there's no indication he ever disbelieved his beloved wife.

The portrait was never again reported to display a lecherous countenance, but other incidents (to be described later) continue until present times.

Jake's career also continued to grow. In 1938, Jake, Beatrice and their two sons left Maine and traveled to Laguna Beach, California, where his art caught the attention of the Harmon-Ising Studio. That job led to his employment by several other top studios including Walt Disney, MGM and Hanna Barbera.

This portrait of Deacon Daniel Day, the patriarch of the Day family in Damariscotta, occupied a position on the wall of an upstairs hallway at the historic Day House. A scantily clad woman walking from down the hall from the shower to a bedroom is said to have observed the portrait to crack a wee smile as she passed by his view. *Portrait courtesy of Sandi Day, photo by Greg Latimer.*

While working for the Disney studio, Jake convinced Walt Disney that Bambi should be a whitetailed deer (native to forest areas) and not a mule deer (more prevalent in the western chaparral). Jake then arranged for two orphaned Maine deer, Bambi and Faline, to be shipped to California as models for the illustrators. During production, Disney commissioned Jake and his closest friend, Lester Hall, to photograph the flora and fauna in the Katahdin, Maine region for the upcoming *Bambi* movie. As a result, many of the scenes and wildlife in *Bambi* are from the Baxter Park area.

After the release of the film *Bambi* in 1942, the Day family began to long for their home in Damariscotta and returned there in 1944. Jake continued to create artwork in many mediums, including painting, woodcarving, photography and more.

His work is still available in the quaint Maine Art Gallery next door to the Day House on Bristol Road, and apparently there are still paranormal presences at play in the gallery and household, according to Sandi Day, the family descendant who supervises the buildings today. "Whatever is here is whimsical and friendly," Sandi said, which are perhaps coincidentally words she also uses to describe Jake, who passed away in 1983.

The "Imaginative" room at the Maine Art Prints gallery on Bristol Road in Damariscotta, where a visitor heard a voice whisper, "Slow down and look." The phrase was a favorite of Maurice "Jake" Day, a renowned illustrator who lived in the building and whose works are still on display at the gallery. Day is also known as "Maine's Bambi connection" for his work as a Walt Disney cartoonist on the Bambi movie. He brought two live deer from Maine to Hollywood to be the models for Bambi, as well as numerous photos of Maine woods and wildlife that contributed to the film's illustrations. *Photo by Greg Latimer.*

Sandi describes several recent incidents. One visitor to the Day House said that it sounded like there was activity upstairs when the area was unoccupied. Another visitor to the location, who said she was sensitive to the paranormal, told Sandi that there was a spirit in the building she described as "happy and fun loving."

A visitor to the gallery who was in the "Imaginative" room specifically heard a male voice whisper in her ear, "Slow down and look," a favorite phrase of Jake.

While it appears there's a possibility that the playful spirit at work in the Day House may be associated with Jake, there have been no additional incidents involving the painting of Daniel Day, which is now in storage.

When the painting was removed recently for a photo, the dour look on the patriarch's face was still there. Of course, on this particular occasion, everyone was properly dressed in the presence of the Voyeur Portrait.

Chapter 21

THE HEADLESS NATIVE AMERICAN GHOST OF WISCASSET

Every day, thousands of motorists pass a scenic, water-filled gully on U.S. Route 1 near the intersection with Flood Street near Old Bath Road. During the daylight hours, they may spot a feeding egret or perhaps a woodchuck scampering along the wooded banks. During the nighttime and early morning hours, some say they've seen a headless ghost clad in Native American attire that appears to be casting about with his arms to search for something in the shallow water and brush.

The locals will tell you that the unfortunate Native American is searching for his lost head. According to the stories passed down, along with historical record, the Native American was part of a raiding party that took part in one of the many sharp, violent skirmishes that occurred when Wiscasset was resettled in 1730 after King Philip's War.

The Native Americans, most likely from the Abenaki tribe, began their assault just after dawn, arriving in canoes and snaking their way around Squam's Island (now Westport Island). They came ashore quietly on a beach near Fort Hill and were able to surprise the garrison of settlers there.

Of the two guards on duty outside the stockade, one was killed outright while the other fled in panic, reaching the fort and sounding an alarm.

The garrison defenders were able to muster quickly, loading and firing two cannons, which caused the Native Americans to retreat.

Positioning their militia to cut the Native Americans off from escape to the river, the settlers started advancing through the woods in the direction of the gully, following the Abenakis as they fell back.

This small glen near Route 1 in Wiscasset has a historic tale of tragedy and of haunting. Residents of the area have reported observing the headless ghost of a Native American who was killed in a battle at the site. These observers feel he is searching for the head he lost in the battle. *Photo by Greg Latimer.*

The Native Americans chose an unfortunate route for their retreat. Advancing toward them was a second group of militia from nearby Dresden whose men had heard the commotion and had quickly armed themselves to assist their fellow settlers. Unbeknownst to the fleeing Native Americans, they were caught right between the militia groups.

The culminating action was fought when the Abenakis found themselves in the low ground near the gully just as the militias arrived at the high ground surrounding it. Battle cries were likely sounded from both sides followed by the staccato discharge of muskets. When the smoke cleared, the Abenakis had vanished into the woods, leaving behind one casualty: a Native American whose head had been blown clean away by a musket shot.

Staring aghast, the militiamen watched as the headless body sank slowly into the murky water of the lagoon. Apparently deciding to leave well enough alone, the settlers declined to search the watery gully and instead let the muddy bottom be the final resting place for the headless Native American. The settlers also lost their desire to pursue the remaining Abenakis deeper into the woods, and the men retired to their garrison.

There may be a compelling reason for the ghost of the doomed Abenaki to haunt this scenic gully in search of his lost head. It is a widespread belief that Native Americans believe that their body must be interred either whole or with all of the parts present.

Widespread beliefs, however, especially about Native American culture, may often and more realistically be considered widespread distortions.

Many western movies, such as *The Searchers* with John Wayne, lend their assertion that Native Americans are unable to pass into the afterlife without all of their body parts, therefore justifying mutilation of their bodies by the cowboys in the film.

There is even a popular legend about Osceola, a leader of the Seminole tribe in Florida during the early 1800s, being executed by authorities at the St. Augustine fortress by beheading. The legend asserts that Osceola's ghost continues to haunt the fort searching for his severed head so he can pass on into the afterlife. This story is repeated many times a night on the numerous walking tours in old town St. Augustine, and it's likely that thousands of people have heard and believed it.

However, it is a well-established fact that Osceola died of natural causes in 1838 at Fort Moultrie, South Carolina, and that he was all in one piece right up to his interment.

In an effort to avoid such a misunderstanding with our hapless headless Native American in Wiscasset, additional research was undertaken. Chasing down the traditions for each individual tribe, especially traditions from the 1700s, was virtually impossible. Instead, the research led to medical professionals who presently work with Native American populations.

In her book *The Nurse as Educator*, Susan Bastable describes the belief that a body should be as intact as possible for burial as a "core value" that is one of few elements common to most Native American cultures. She counsels nurses to expect that Native Americans will want amputated limbs to be retained and preserved, as they "usually want to reclaim amputated body parts for burial."

Another nurse, Jean Ann Cantore, allows for more detail of this custom in a posting on minoritynurse.com, where she wrote:

> *One Pima belief that is shared by several other tribes is that any body part that is removed during life, such as by amputation, must be put back with the body when a person dies. Otherwise, the person will go on to the afterlife incomplete. In Papago (Tohono O'odham) culture, when a person dies, the family bathes the body and combs his or her hair. All hair that comes out*

in the brush or on the floor must be bound and placed with the body so the spirits will take the deceased person with them.

If the Abenaki killed in Wiscasset held these beliefs to be true, then no wonder he continues to haunt the watery gully so desperately seeking his lost head—his eternity depends on finding it.

Motorists passing by this quiet gully at night may want to glance over to see if they can catch a glimpse of his apparition, or they may just want to wish the poor soul good luck in his unending search.

Chapter 22

THE HAUNTED LIGHTHOUSE OF PEMAQUID POINT

The Pemaquid Point Lighthouse, towering over the crashing surf on a rocky ledge, has been the scene of both history and haunts. Tragedy first visited this shoreline in 1635, well before the lighthouse was built, and it may be that one or more of the victims in this tragedy still haunts the area.

The *Angel Gabriel* was a 250-ton galleon carrying colonists and supplies from England to the settlement at Pemaquid, near the Pemaquid Point Lighthouse. Once reaching the harbor, she was able to anchor and began disembarking her passengers and cargo.

Unfortunately, a major hurricane blew in from the southeast while an unknown number of passengers and crew were still aboard the ship. While the record is unclear, apparently all or most of those left aboard perished as the ship broke up in the angry surf and unforgiving rocks.

If one of those lost passengers was an elderly woman, that may explain the presence of an apparition seen a number of times on the point and in the lighthouse area. Witnesses report seeing a water-soaked white-haired woman clad in a white dress and clasping a red shawl around her shoulders. She appears to be in distress, frantically searching about the area as though seeking assistance. Sometimes she is seen shivering in the museum section of the keeper's house.

Another paranormal report that may be associated with the sinking of the *Angel Gabriel* is that of screaming and cries of distress echoing up to the shoreline from the churning ocean. However, tragedy is a frequent visitor to this scenic point, and it is not uncommon for local rescue crews to be called

The historic Pemaquid Point Lighthouse in Bristol is the beacon that guards the tip of the Pemaquid Peninsula. It was the lighthouse chosen to represent the state when the United States Treasury minted the Maine state quarter, and it is also home to numerous paranormal incidents. *Photo by Greg Latimer.*

to the area for a boat in distress or a sightseer swept off the rocks and into the sea by a chance wave. Perhaps the lonely cries for help come from a collection of souls who perished on this rocky point.

Other paranormal phenomena continue to manifest at the location. A woman who was visiting the area at night reported seeing every light in the unoccupied building housing the museum and keeper's house suddenly turn on all at once, something that would be impossible using the light switches for each room in the three-story structure.

A recent paranormal exploration conducted by the Mysterious Destinations Team noted electromagnetic field (EMF) spikes at a number of locations in the facility, a potential indicator of paranormal activity. They also had a response to a question about whether they were welcome at the building when a flashlight turned on to indicate that they were not.

Perhaps the most compelling and continuous evidence can be found documented in the guest book for the apartment in the keeper's house that is available for weekly rentals during the summer. (That's right, you can stay in a haunted lighthouse on the Maine coast, with a portion of the rental fee used to maintain the lighthouse. To learn more, contact Newcastle Square Vacation Rentals in Damariscotta.)

These descriptions are particularly interesting because most of the people reporting them are simply there to enjoy their stay, not to experience paranormal activity.

Some of the reports are relatively straightforward, such as this entry by a couple from Connecticut: "Only heard a ghost once, at 3:10 a.m. slamming a door downstairs."

Others are quite a bit more striking and so detailed that it is hard to imagine how they could have been made up. "Heard a female voice singing, with classical music playing," wrote a visitor from New York, adding, "I had goosebumps on goosebumps!"

Some reports involve renters who have heard the stories and included their own paranormal detection equipment in their travel bags. A woman who brought a K2 meter, used to detect anomalies in EMF activity, reported wild fluctuations on her meter while staying in the apartment.

Aside from the scenic vista and dynamic structure that is the Pemaquid Point Light, what is most attractive about this location is its accessibility. The lighthouse area includes a park, an art gallery, a museum and plenty of parking. The light tower is also accessible during summer daylight hours through a guided tour provided by local volunteers. This scenic light, chosen by the U.S. Treasury to be featured on the quarter dedicated to the State of Maine, is just a thirty-minute ride down Route 130 from Damariscotta. There is a nominal charge for parking in the summer months, and more can be learned about the facility by visiting bristolparks.org/lighthouse.

The picturesque light has attracted many artists, including Edward Hopper, who captured its image in his 1929 watercolor *Pemaquid Light*. Today, Pemaquid Point is one of New England's most visited and photographed lighthouses, drawing over 100,000 visitors annually.

An extensive restoration in 2007 has kept the Pemaquid Light tower gleaming in the sun. The tower's interior brick veneer, which was added

> Sept. 20-27, 2008
> What a perfect week - Sat. thru Thurs. - bright sun, mild breezes. Pure relaxation! Our car didn't move much all week. This was my 50th year visiting the Pemaquid area. Interesting to stay at the keeper's quarters — only heard a ghost once at 3:10 a.m. slamming a door downstairs

"Only heard a ghost once, at 3:10 a.m. slamming a door downstairs" declares this entry in the Pemaquid Point Lighthouse guest book. *Photo by Greg Latimer.*

Tuesday, May 28, 2012

We arrived on Saturday after nearly 8½ hours from our departure in Southern New York State. There are no words to describe the beauty and wildness of the sea and this incredible Keeper's Apartment! Each day has been an increasing adventure! On our first night here we heard a loud bump and "slam" downstairs about 11 pm. I stopped in front of the stairs and heard a female voice singing with classical music playing. I had goosebumps on goosebumps! My husband did not hear anything. Have not had a repeat experience and that's OK. I asked the museum caretaker, Chas, about this and he laughed and said, "Oh, that's probably just the old lighthouse keeper - and his wife (?). I saw in a previous journal a notation about the tenants' hearing a door slam downstairs, and couldn't help but think it was a ghost... maybe not ☺"

We have experienced a fabulous, glorious thunderstorm that shook the windows! The sea has been green, blue, grey and almost black in the dark storm. It is alive with beauty and mystery. It will be our 43rd Wedding Anniversary on May 31st, and it all our years of being together! This is the most wondrous place we have ever been to. It will be difficult to leave next Saturday, indeed. We will be back —

This page from the guest book at the Pemaquid Point Lighthouse includes a report of hearing "a female voice singing, with classical music playing," adding, "I had goosebumps on goosebumps!" *Photo by Greg Latimer.*

along with the cast-iron staircase during the mid- to late nineteenth century, was restored in 2010.

The park and museum are managed by the Town of Bristol and the Bristol Lighthouse Committee. The light tower is managed by the American Lighthouse Foundation.

The park is presently open twenty-four hours a day (of course, the buildings are closed), so who knows what a nighttime visitor might witness. An apparitional lady in a red shawl? House lights turning themselves on? Or, if one listens carefully to the ocean beyond the pounding surf line, are they hearing the cries of seagulls on the night breeze, or the phantom screams of stricken sailors as they struggle against fate in the dark, unforgiving sea?

BIBLIOGRAPHY

African Repository of the American Colonization Society. Washington, D.C.: C. Alexander, Printer, 1854.

Aleccia, JoNel. "60 Years in an Iron Lung: US Polio Survivor Worries about New Global Threat." New York, NY. National Broadcasting Corporation, nbcnews.com, 2013.

Anderson, Kraig. "Pemaquid Point, ME." www.lighthousefriends.com.

Bastable, Susan B. *The Nurse as Educator.* Sudbury, MA: Jones & Bartlett Publishers, 2008.

Batignani, Karen. *Maine's Coastal Cemeteries: A Historic Tour.* Rockport, ME: Down East Books, 2003.

Bergad, Laird W. *Cuban Rural Society in the Nineteenth Century: The Social and Economic History of Monoculture in Matanzas.* Princeton, NJ: Princeton University Press, 1990.

Blanchard, Dorothy. *Along the Damariscotta.* Mt. Pleasant, SC: Arcadia Publishing, 1995.

Boatner, Colonel Mark Mayo, III. "Life Guard of Washington." In *An Encyclopedia of the American Revolution.* Philadelphia, PA. David McKay Company, 1966; revised, 1974.

Braude, Ann. *Radical Spirits: Spiritualism and Women's Rights in Nineteenth-Century America, Second Edition.* Bloomington: Indiana University Press, 2001.

Bulkeley, Ben. "The Ghost Island." *Boothbay Register,* October 26, 2012.

———. "An Island Apart." *Boothbay Register,* September 27, 2012.

Cantore, Jean Ann. "Earth, Wind, Fire and Water." www.minoritynurse.com.

Cartland, John Henry. *Ten Years at Pemaquid: Sketches of Its History and Its Ruins.* Pemaquid Beach, ME: 1899.

Cartwright, Steve. "Living Aboard: Damariscove Harbor Was a Family's Home for 16 Years." *The Working Waterfront,* May 1, 2003.

Castner, Harold W. The Castner Files. Collection at Skidompha Library, Damariscotta, ME.

———. "A History of Banking in Newcastle and Damariscotta." Damariscotta, ME: unpublished manuscript, 1960.

———. *The Smile of the Patriarch.* In the Castner Files, Collection at Skidompha Library, Damariscotta, ME.

Chase, Fanny S. *Wiscasset in Pownalborough: A History of the Shire Town and the Salient Historical Features of the Territory Between the Sheepscot and Kennebec Rivers.* Wiscasset, ME: 1941.

Christie, Josh. "It's Worth the Trip: Plenty to Please Day Hikers near Damariscotta River." *Portland Press Herald,* July 10, 2011.

Cushman, Reverend David Quimby. *The History of Ancient Sheepscot and Newcastle.* Bath, ME: E. Upton & Son, Printers, 1883.

Damariscove Island Lands in Good Hands. Brunswick, ME: Maine Chapter of the Nature Conservancy, 2005.

Damariscove Trail Guide and History. Boothbay Harbor, ME: Boothbay Region Land Trust, undated.

Dejean, Edmee. *Images of America: Damariscotta Lake.* Mt. Pleasant, SC: Arcadia Publishing, 2011.

Department of Maine Resources. "The Maine Eel and Elver Fishery." www.maine.gov.

Dodge, Marjorie and Calvin Dodge. "Damariscotta History: History of Alna Lodge 1854–1880, Part III." *The Lincoln County News,* February 18, 2009.

"Dodge Point Project Description." www.state.me.us.

Dunbar, Olivia Howard. "Authors at Home, XXXI: Blanche Willis Howard in Dresden." *New York Times,* July 16, 1898.

Duncan, Roger F. *Coastal Maine: A Maritime History.* Woodstock, VT: Countryman Press, 1992.

"Four of Maine's Historic Old Homesteads." *Lewiston (ME) Evening Journal,* September 16, 1899.

Frauenthal, Henry, MD, and Jacolyn Manning, MD. *Manual of Infantile Paralysis, with Modern Methods of Treatment.* Philadelphia, PA: F.A. Davis Co., 1914.

Frink, Martha C. "Kavanaugh and Cottrill: Newcastle's 18th Century Entrepreneurs." *Midcoast Review,* April 2003.

Gay, Maude Clark. *Garden of the East: Wiscasset on Sheepscot Bay, Trail of the Maine Pioneer Women.* Lewiston, ME: Lewiston Journal Co., 1916.

Gibson, John. *50 Hikes in Coastal and Inland Maine.* Woodstock, VT: Countryman Press, 2008.

Godfrey, Carlos Emmor, MD. *The Commander-in-Chief's Guard.* Washington, D.C.: Stevenson-Smith Company, 1904.

Gregg, W.P., and Benjamin Pond. *Charter of the Penobscot and Kennebec Railroad Company.* Boston, MA: Railroad Laws and Charters of the United States, Charles Little and James Brown (publishers), 1851.

Griffin, Carl Russell, and Alaric Faulkner. *Coming of Age on Damariscove Island, Maine.* Orono, ME: Northeast Folklore Society, 1981.

Hauck, Dennis William. *Haunted Places: The National Directory.* New York: Penguin Books, 2002.

Hogarty, Patricia. "Use Your Peripheral Vision at the Whitney's Ghost Bar." www.examiner.com, January 24, 2010.

"Hortense and Henry Ferne II Memorial Fine Arts Room." www.wiscasset.lib.me.us.

James, Edward T., ed. *Notable American Women: A Biographical Dictionary, 1607–1950.* Vol. 2. Cambridge, MA: Belknap Press of Harvard University Press, 1971.

Krystek, Lee. "Spook Lights." www.unmuseum.org.

Latimer, Greg. "Object Photographed Over Newcastle Remains Unidentified." *The Lincoln County News*, February 13, 2014.

————. *Past and Present in the Twin Villages of Damariscotta and Newcastle.* Damariscotta, ME: Lincoln County Publishing Co., 2000.

Lincoln County News, December 22 and December 29, 1882.

Lowndes, Marion. *Ghosts That Still Walk the Earth.* New York: Knopf, 1943.

Maine Ghost Hunters Presents: ZeroLux Radio—Carly Masterson. Radio interview. www.maineghosthunters.org.

Maine Island Trail Guide. Portland, ME: Maine Island Trail Association, 2010.

Massachusetts Soldiers and Sailors of the Revolutionary War. Boston: Wright and Potter Printing Company, State Printers, 1896.

Merchant Vessels of the United States. Washington, D.C.: U.S. Department of Transportation, 1915.

Michaud, Kelly. "Midcoast Offers Lots of Haunts." *Rockland (ME) Courier Gazette*, October 2004.

Miller, Aaron C. "Ghostly Stories in Wiscasset." *Wiscasset (ME) Newspaper*, October 2002.

Morgan, Janet. "Library Ghost?" www.mainecrimewriters.com.

New York Times. "Maurice E. Day, Animator, 90; Drew Deer for Movie 'Bambi.'" May 19, 1983.

———. "Obituary notice—Blanche Willis Howard." October 10, 1898.

"Polio—Fact Sheet for Parents." cdc.gov, 2013.

Proceedings of the Wiscasset Fire Society. Wiscasset, ME. Reprinted from *The Sheepscot Echo*, 1908.

"Recorded donations." *Baptist Missionary Magazine* 35 (1855).

Riess, Warren. *The Angel Gabriel: The Elusive English Galleon.* Damariscotta, ME: Lincoln County Publishing Co., 2001.

Roberts, Paula. *On the Trail in Lincoln County.* Damariscotta, ME: Lincoln County Publishing Co., 2006.

Rolde, Neil. *Maine: A Narrative History.* Harpswell, ME: Harpswell Press, 1990.

Scofield, John. "Character Marks the Coast of Maine." *National Geographic Magazine* 133, no. 4 (June 1968).

Shephard, Kathy, and Robb Phillips. "And You Just Thought You Were Alone in the House!" Paranormal Technology Investigations, www.tcprs.com.

Silver, Alexandra. *Polio Epidemic of 1916.* Time Inc. Time.com, Tuesday, October 26, 2010.

Sobel, Robert, and John Raimo. *Biographical Directory of the Governors of the United States, 1789–1978.* Westport, CT: Greenwood Press, 1988.

Soldier Details, Kingsbury, John H. Washington, D.C. National Park Service, Civil War Index, www.nps.gov, 2014.

Thompson, Winfield. "Damariscove." *New England Magazine* 11 (1895).

Thorsell, Erika. "Ancient Legends of the Swamp Lights." www.maineghosthunters.org.

Town of Wiscasset. "Welcome to Wiscasset's Community Trails!" www.wiscasset.org.

Varney, Geo. J. "History of Wiscasset, Maine." *A Gazetteer of the State of Maine*, 1886.

Waite, Lea. "Colonial Maine—Earlier Than You May Have Imagined." www.mainecrimewriters.com.

William T. Glidden-Austin Block, Newcastle, Lincoln County, ME. Washington, D.C. Historic American Buildings Survey, Library of Congress (documentation compiled after 1933).

Wilson, Alexandra, comp. *The Shoestring Guide of Lincoln County.* Damariscotta, ME: Lincoln County Publishing Co., 2005.

ABOUT THE AUTHOR

Greg Latimer has been seeking answers since he first started as a newspaper reporter at the age of sixteen. By age eighteen, he was a full-time reporter/photographer for a newspaper in Los Angeles. It was only several years later that he moved up to the position of investigative reporter for the daily *Los Angeles Herald Examiner*, where he established his reputation through his coverage of the infamous torture-murders committed by Roy Lewis Norris and Lawrence Sigmund Bittaker.

His fact-based investigative reporting came to the attention of a detective lieutenant with the police department in Hermosa Beach, California (located in southwest Los Angeles County), and Latimer was recruited as a police evidence photographer. Here he received special training in evidence photography and crime scene evidence procedure. He documented hundreds of crime scenes and testified in a number of felony cases, including a homicide.

After some years there, he returned to journalism but continued to work with several former Hermosa Beach Police officers as a private investigator's agent, collecting both photographic and video evidence, preparing the evidence for court and testifying about that evidence in trials.

Latimer presently resides in Maine, where his articles and photos continue to be published in *The Lincoln County News*. He is also the research director for MysteriousDestinationsMagazine.com, an online publication that explores mysteries in the United States and Caribbean. In 2001, he was recognized by the New England Press Association with an award for investigative reporting.

For additional photos, videos and information regarding the chapters in this book, please visit MysteriousDestinationsMagazine.com and click on the "New Book: Haunted Damariscotta" tile located on the left side of the home page.

Visit us at
www.historypress.net

....

This title is also available as an e-book